STOP THE STRESS IN SCHOOLS

Mental health strategies teachers can use to build
a kinder gentler classroom

Joey Mandel

Pembroke Publishers Limited

To Ella and Jeannie, who show strength every day.

© 2014 Pembroke Publishers
538 Hood Road
Markham, Ontario, Canada L3R 3K9
www.pembrokepublishers.com

Distributed in the U.S. by Stenhouse Publishers
480 Congress Street
Portland, ME 04101
www.stenhouse.com

All rights reserved.
No part of this publication may be reproduced in any form or by any means electronic or mechanical, including photocopy, scanning, recording, or any information, storage or retrieval system, without permission in writing from the publisher. Excerpts from this publication may be reproduced under licence from Access Copyright, or with the express written permission of Pembroke Publishers Limited, or as permitted by law.

Every effort has been made to contact copyright holders for permission to reproduce borrowed material. The publishers apologize for any such omissions and will be pleased to rectify them in subsequent reprints of the book.

We acknowledge the financial support of the Government of Canada through the Canada Book Fund (CBF) for our publishing activities.

We acknowledge the assistance of the Government of Ontario through the Ontario Media Development Corporation's Ontario Book Initiative.

Library and Archives Canada Cataloguing in Publication

Mandel, Joey, author
   Stop the stress in schools : mental health strategies teachers can use to build a kinder, gentler classroom / Joey Mandel.

Includes bibliographical references and index.
Issued in print and electronic formats.
ISBN 978-1-55138-298-2 (pbk.).--ISBN 978-1-55138-900-4 (pdf)

   1. Classroom environment--Psychological aspects. 2. Stress in children--Prevention. 3. Stress management for children--Study and teaching (Elementary). I. Title.

LB3013.25.M36 2014   371.102'4   C2014-902870-9
                                       C2014-902871-7

Editor: Kat Mototsune
Cover Design: John Zehethofer
Typesetting: Jay Tee Graphics Ltd.

Printed and bound in Canada
9 8 7 6 5 4 3 2 1

Contents

Introduction *5*

    The Stress Effect *6*
    Mental Health Strategies in the Classroom *8*
    Stopping the Stress *9*

Chapter 1: Creating a Positive Classroom *11*

    Relationship Dynamics *12*
    Teacher Relationships *12*
        Teacher–Self *12*
        Teacher–Teacher *13*
        Teacher–Class *13*
        Teacher–Student *14*
    Student Relationships *14*
        Student–Self *15*
        Student–Student *15*
        Student–Class *16*
        Class–Student *16*

Chapter 2: Giving Positive Response *18*

    Acting on Student Behavior *18*
        Ignore *19*
        React *19*
        Respond *20*
    The Positive Response Process *20*
        Give Feedback *21*
        Set Goals *21*
        Regulate *22*
        Engage *23*
        Support *23*
    Social-Emotional Character Traits *25*
        Awareness *26*
        Acceptance *26*
        Ability to Manage Stress *26*

Chapter 3: Awareness *27*

    Of Strengths *27*
    Of Challenges *33*
    Of Strengths and Challenges of Others *36*
    Of Triggers *39*
    Of Impact of Stress on the Body *45*
    Of Impact of Stress on Behavior *51*
    Of Impact of Stress on Thinking *56*
    Of Impact of Stress on Feelings *60*

Chapter 4: Acceptance *67*

    Of Self *67*
    Of Others *69*
    Of the Situation *72*
    Of the Thinking of Others *77*
    Of the Need to Adapt *85*
    Of the Behavior of Others *90*

Chapter 5: Ability to Manage Stress *95*

    Self-Calming *95*
    Changing the Way We Think *102*
    Changing the Way Others Feel *106*
    Going Back and Trying Again *112*
    Applying Strategies *117*

Conclusion *121*
   Acknowledgments *121*
Professional Resources *122*
Index *124*

Introduction

> *I'm Ella. I am 8 years old. I love rabbits and horses. And I love to play with my Dad and my brother and sister. I DON'T love school. This story is about how I am learning to feel more confident and less nervous about going to school. I don't like school. And I will tell you why. The day feels so l-o-n-g. Seven hours feel like a million years to me. I feel like my teacher yells at me all the time when I am too slow at math. And I don't know who to play with at recess. Being at school feels so hard to me even though I know to some kids it is as easy as eating a piece of cake.*

Ella is the eight-year-old daughter of someone I know. She had a lot of difficult feelings, but was unsure why she had them and what she was feeling.

> *Every morning I wake up and I feel very nervous about going to school. My belly rumbles and hurts. My head feels heavy. When my mom drives me to school, getting out of the car is the hardest part of all. She walks me to the door and then I start to cry. I can't think of anything aside from how nervous I feel. With my mom leaving me, I feel lost.*

Ella's body is sending her warning messages; these messages make her feel powerless and incapable. Ella went to see a thinking coach who supports children's understanding of their thoughts and feelings. With the thinking coach, Ella was better able to understand what her body's aches were telling her and what she could do about them.

> *My mom took me to see a thinking coach. She understands what I am feeling. She is trying to help me think differently about what I am thinking.*

With support, Ella learned to identify her worries and the way they made her body feel. She learned to change the way she thought and reacted to her worries.

> *Last year was different. Last year my teacher was l-o-v-e-l-y. Her voice was soft and warm. She made me feel special and loved. Last year I was confident.*
>
> *My teacher this year wants me to be "more independent." "You are a big girl," she keeps telling me in a stern voice. She yells a lot. At me!*

We have a huge role to play in the lives of students like Ella. We can support them and help them respond differently to the world around them. But the first change in response might have to come from us, in our responses to children like Ella.

What does Ella need to be successful? What can we do as a school system to help Ella get to school? What can I do as an educator to help Ella develop into the best version of herself? What skills and self-calming strategies can I teach Ella so that she can feel differently about school? How can I help her be more resilient and optimistic as she faces a world of ever-increasing challenges?

What did Ella really need in order to get to school and feel confident and ready to learn? She needed a kind and calm teacher. She needed someone who loved, supported, and believed in her, someone who was soft and gentle. In my book *Moment-to-Moment*, I write "the most influential commodity a teacher brings to the classroom is his or her own positive personal qualities and warm character in the face of a challenging situation." It seems that as a long as we keep reminding ourselves of that one commodity we can give children what they really need—our positive support.

If we want to provide safe and caring school communities, if we want positive emotional climates in our schools that reduce stress on children, professional development should centre on helping teachers maintain their positive personal qualities and warm character in the face of stress. It is often the case that teachers are kind and gentle most of the time, yet when under stress (and teaching is a stressful job) they can lose those kind and gentle qualities. They sometimes turn to reactive—aggressive, critical, harsh—strategies. And it is important to note that reactive and aggressive strategies are often successful in the short term. For both teachers and students, these reactions often work. Loud, harsh, disruptive, violent aggression gives anyone an immediate voice. People stop; people listen; people react and move in. You are not being listened to when you are not being heard; if you yell, if you break down, if you cry or scream, people respond to your needs. Children listen to the screaming teacher and teachers attend to the aggressive child. But these strategies are contrary to the skills we want to teach our students.

Teachers need support in developing a process that creates a kind and gentle classroom, one they can sustain even during the hard moments. They need the skills to remain calm in the face of their increasingly demanding and stressful role as educators, counselors, and mentors; the skills to protect themselves from burnout and disillusion in a job that seems to consistently demand more and more of them. We need to encourage teachers to support each other as much as they support their students, so that teachers are working in a kind and gentle environment as much as they are teaching in one.

The Stress Effect

Stress is a natural reaction to threats in the environment. Our bodies are programmed to seek out danger in the environment and to respond in self-preservation. Perceived threats to our survival—dangerous animals, enemies, violent weather—trigger a fear response. In today's classroom, the trigger can be a math test, an annoying noise, or worrying that you have hurt someone's feelings. If these fear responses are being sensed regularly, they can cause physical and cognitive disruption.

The part of our brains involved in stress is the amygdala, with its primary role in processing our emotional reactions. The amygdala stores memories associated with emotional events and senses warnings throughout the body that there is danger in the environment. When danger is sensed, the amygdala sends stress hormones to prepare the body to face the danger, run from it, or remain perfectly still. In this state of Fight, Flight, or Freeze, all the body's resources are available for survival as it moves into a ready-to-react state: increased heart rate and perspiration; eyes open to seek danger.

When the body is in a state of Fight, Flight, or Freeze, its cognitive capacity is shut down. Pathways to the neocortex—the part of the brain responsible for rational thought, impulse control, and assessment of consequences—shut off to conserve energy for reaction and protection. For students, school functioning occurs in the neocortex. When pathways to the neocortex shut down, the logic, impulse control, problem-solving, and language abilities of the brain either do not work or do not work as well.

Stress triggers in the environment cause internal feelings of discomfort, but everyone has different behavioral reactions to these triggers. Some people use the charged-up internal energy to jump in, get everything done, take over, control, plan, organize, and execute a task; others pull away from the task, not sure where to begin.

Triggers are not always innately negative. They can be objects or events that are positive and exciting. Students might become so involved in an activity that their bodies become overstimulated and send distress warnings. Children can experience sensory overload to positive events and enjoyable environments. Or students can want something so much (e.g., a cookie or a video game) that they become worried by thinking they will not get it, jealous that someone else's will be better, or angry because they think someone else will get more.

It is easiest to view stress in three levels—high, medium, and low—or as three stages on a Stress Curve (see page 8), on which the upward arc reflects the increase in stress we experience as we move from a state of low to high stress.

- Low-stress environments expose individuals to small, age-appropriate triggers that are manageable. The person faces the trigger (e.g., a task or activity), manages it, and experiences success with it. Success does not necessarily mean that the person accomplished the task perfectly, but that the task was undertaken and there was some positive closure to the event.

- Medium stress is experienced by an individual facing a trigger or multiple triggers that start to demand more skills and abilities than he/she might have. The person begins to use a lot of energy to handle and manage tasks or triggers, and this begins to deplete his/her internal resources.

- Levels of high stress exist when there is one large trigger or multiple smaller triggers that demand more of an individual than he/she has the skills to manage. High stress and prolonged periods of medium stress begin to affect a person through a depletion of physical and mental resources in the person's attempt to deal with and manage stress.

The Fight, Flight, or Freeze reaction is functional when there is real danger (e.g., fire or tigers), since the person needs to respond quickly and efficiently. A Fight, Flight, or Freeze reaction to daily stresses is not functional and reduces a person's ongoing capacity to problem-solve and learn.

> The medium level of stress is the key time when each student's behavior, thoughts, and feelings vary.

STRESS CURVE

Stress Curve

High Stress
- Fight, flight, or freeze
- Body: Dysregulated
- Can't learn
- 💭 I can't
- ♡ sad, angry, nervous

Medium Stress
- Body: Warning signs

Low Stress
- Body: Relaxed
- Able to learn
- 💭 I can
- ♡ Able

Use the Stress Curve as you begin to talk about, examine, and manage stress with students. After providing a few examples of Thinking and Feeling, brainstorm the area of Medium Stress with students. The Medium Stress area is the one in which students are likely to have different behaviors, thoughts, and feelings based on the situation, the trigger, and their personal abilities to manage challenging situations. There are many effective calming strategies that allow teachers and students to face stress and manage it without running away from fear, avoiding challenges, or acting against each other.

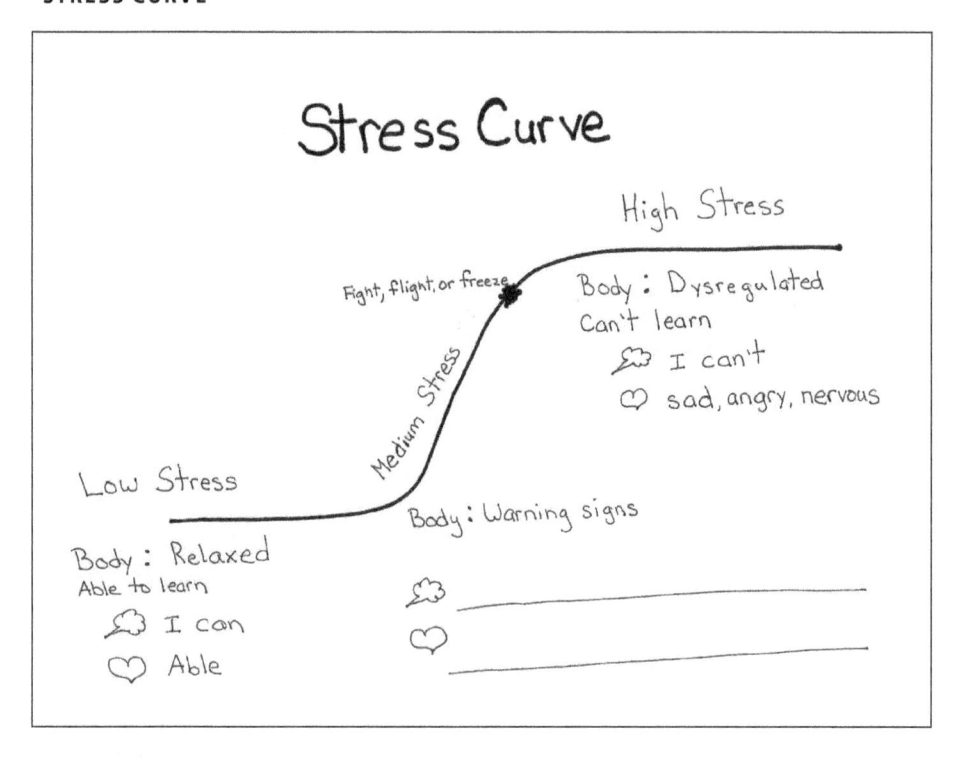

> Skills in this case are not simply intellectual skills needed to succeed academically, but are abilities necessary to accomplish a task and to handle the stress of the task; e.g., self-calming skills.

Mental Health Strategies in the Classroom

About 20% of children struggle with true mental health challenges that interfere with their daily learning and their social and academic success (Waddell et al., 2002). In many school systems, there is professional support offered to students who clearly have mental health issues. Effective evidence-based mental health strategies provide individuals with the ability to reduce and manage the stress that increases the severity of symptoms of many mental health challenges. These strategies improve the quality of lives of individuals with or without mental illness by giving them the tools to be aware of stress, to understand the personal impact stress has on them, and to learn effective ways of managing their stress. The impact of these mental health strategies is increased personal well-being and success. Teachers need to seek assistance for students with mental health challenges, because these supports often have positive results.

> A teacher's role is not to diagnose or treat children with mental illness, but to identify the children who need special services and to learn basic strategies to support them in the classroom.

But there is a large group of students who are not diagnosed with mental illnesses yet still struggle, students who do not have the social-emotional tools to deal with stressors. These students often do not get the understanding and support they need. They will likely never get therapy or counselling, simply because there is no apparent need for it. These children might struggle, but the effects are not overwhelming or disconcerting. They are the children who, if life does not include too many big, stressful events, will be able to manage and get by in their life's journey. However, if life throws them a big stressor or a few too many little stressors, these children might not have the tools that will allow them to rise to those challenges and succeed. The point at which their social-emotional tools are not up to the challenge might occur in elementary school, or perhaps in high school, or not until they have families of their own they need to provide and care for. But if and when those life stresses come, and if the stressors are too big or they accumulate too much, then these individuals might not have the resiliency skills to recover and the perseverance skills to carry on.

People living in the middle of this continuum of skills struggle throughout their lives, but rarely get the support they need. Although never diagnosed with a form of mental illness, they struggle with social skills, anxiety, chronic sadness, obsessiveness, explosive anger, disorganization, and/or inattentiveness.

These students still struggle with social, emotional, and behavioral challenges, but the challenges are often seen as being within their control. The inability to meet these challenges is often blamed on the individual, who is seen as lazy or "bad," and on his or her parents for being absent or negligent. But if we understand psychological challenges to exist as a spectrum, then it does not make sense to arbitrarily draw a line in the continuum, to determine that a child on one side of the line receives a diagnosis and support but a child on the other side is not serviced.

This is where educators can play a vital role. Teachers can create climates that will affect the lives of the children who struggle but are not in desperate need. We must use the same strategies and techniques for the child we are worried about as we would to support the child with a diagnosis. It is easy for the children who struggle to fall through the cracks. However, using only a little engagement and support, we can make a significant impact in their lives.

Stopping the Stress

Creating a kind and gentle classroom might seem to be a huge undertaking. But most teachers already have an affirmative intent to create a positive space and are using consistent daily energy to sustain it.

It is easy to be kind most of the time, but during stressful moments it is harder. Personal stress affects the job, the stress of work hits, or students push back and are noncompliant—these situations erode a teacher's ability to be kind and gentle. As a key figure in the classroom, the teacher sets the tone for the creation of a positive classroom and healthy relationships within that classroom. If we use and model the positive coping strategies we want our students to use, we become a part of the social-emotional process and make an aggregate step in building a positive classroom climate. If we show and model what we expect from students, we close the final link in that positive classroom climate, creating a less stressful environment for our students.

Being kind and gentle does not mean that there should not be consequences in a classroom. As teachers, we need to set a tone that lets children know that actions that are unkind or unsafe will not be tolerated. It is the way we set this tone and apply the principles to our behavior that makes or breaks our ability to truly build authentic positive climates. Children need clear rules and often benefit from clear consequences. Sometimes a child needs to be removed from a situation and to make amends. Following through on consequences does not mean not abiding by our positive approach, as long as the consequences are imposed in a process, with kindness, gentle delivery, and full explanation (at the time or once the child has calmed down).

As teachers, we can truly be successful in these challenging moments only if we have a better awareness and understanding of our own stress and how to regulate our bodies to self-calm. If we, ourselves, use the physical and mental calming strategies that we ask our students to use in their challenging moments, then we will decrease the amount that we react in moments of stress, and will decrease harsh or negative interactions with our students.

These are the challenging moments and the children who make us question our teaching practices and strategies. These are the situations this book will focus on. Some days will go well for us and other days will not, just as for our students. This is the learning experience. And developing guiding principles to manage stress takes the focus off the stress and puts it on the learning experience.

1
Creating a Positive Classroom

Strong, healthy relationships are crucial to emotional well-being. They are protective factors and supports through challenging moments; they are also the creators of the stress and conflict. Either way, they directly influence the way people feel, positively or negatively. Every interaction we have with ourselves and with others has mental-health effects. Every interaction can shape and influence the way we think and feel. We build strong relationships, not only by what we do and say, but also by how we respond to ourselves and others.

We can create a positive classroom climate—one that will maintain high expectations, rules, and routines through a positive teaching approach—by focusing on the relationships within the classroom and the school. For a teacher, this will begin with his/her own relationship to self, and then extend to relationships with others; i.e., colleagues and students. The teacher can attempt to strengthen his/her relationship with students through every interaction, and understand that his/her role is to support students to build positive and strong relationships with each other. We need to consistently guide children to examine the way they are treating one another and to support their interactions: to help them interact with one another in positive ways; not to correct or to discipline, but to guide them without judgment through interaction and problem-solving. We want to teach children to think of their actions and the consequences of those actions for themselves and others.

A positive classroom requires there to be a process with students, a thoughtful way of acting when a student is unkind to another. It is not just about filling the room with list of rules: e.g., *Don't run, Don't be rude, Be kind, Be positive*. We all know that these rules do not work in isolation. These rules assume that children know what being kind looks like and that they can be kind even when they are upset. They assume that when a child is very frustrated he/she can calm down and be respectful. If a child is reactive and explosive, even if that child makes the school pledge, he/she will be unable to maintain it when experiencing distress. This will lead to feelings of shame and guilt at being unable to fulfil promises made.

These rules also assume that teachers themselves are being positive toward their students. Most teachers are kind and empathetic—it's one reason they were drawn to teaching. Yet the stresses of the job create situations in which teachers lose their ability to maintain self-control and they, too, react with emotion to challenging situations. In order to build positive relationships, we must first and foremost be willing to examine and internalize the processes we are striving to teach children. Everything that we want to teach and instil in the children should be modeled and attempted first ourselves.

Interpersonal dynamics are complex and multi-layered. If we want to create a positive classroom climate, we need to ensure that we are supporting a positive schoolwide climate. That climate exists in multiple interpersonal relationships. If we miss one, then the community weakens, not just because of a missing link, but also as a result of the inconsistency of messages and relationships. Inequality in one relationship will cause inequality in the others.

Relationship Dynamics

Our role as teachers is to begin to be aware of the different relationships and dynamics that we create. Where are the dynamics strong within our school and our classroom, and in what we contribute to them? Where are they weak? Understanding the different relationships will allow us to know where energy needs to be placed to build those relationships and improve upon them.

Ask yourself: *What role do I play in the positive or negative construction of relationships in my school? How do I respond with interpersonal dynamics in general? How do I respond to them when I am under stress?* It is often easy to examine a scenario that is not related to us and to immediately know the proper, kind, and functional way of behaving; however, we don't always respond that way when we are under stress, when it involves staff with whom we struggle to maintain positive relationships, or with a student who is misbehaving.

> **Throughout the book, we examine the ways in which what seem to be obvious and functional ways of interacting positively with others can break down. Relationship boxes show how each trait can manifest itself in terms of interpersonal relationships.**

Teacher Relationships

Step back and appreciate the power you have in the classroom over the mood and well-being of yourself and your students. Every action you take has the power to modify the way you feel, think, and act about yourself and others, and the way your students feel, think, and act about themselves and others. Teachers must be able to monitor their own behavior, thoughts, and feelings. They must be able to examine how they act in a given situation and what those actions are based on.

Teacher–Self

As a teacher, your first relationship is actually with yourself. Without prioritizing a healthy internal relationship and control over your own thoughts and feelings, it is impossible to respond in kindness and gently support the needs of others. Teachers must be able to examine how they feel about themselves, how they handle the pressures of the workload and the demands that a roomful of children places on them. Once teachers learn personal self-calming and stress-management strategies, they will be in a position to act in a more responsive way toward their students.

> You mess up your report comments, and that affects your report cards and those of others on the staff. What action do you take? Does it build positive relationships?
> - You apologize to your principal and staff members and move on.
>   Yes: You deal with the problem and then put it out of your mind.

- You apologize to your principal and the staff members, but you go home at night and replay the situation over and over in your head, rethinking how you could have prevented it.
  No: By fixating on the problem, you are increasing your stress and making the problem bigger.
- You blame another teacher for an aspect of the problem that was his/her fault.
  No: Creating a culture of blame does not help staff relationships and does not model the message we send to students—that mistakes happen and should be forgiven.
- You say nothing and keep working.
  No: Your lack of ownership and responsibility can leave others feeling that the process was not complete and blaming you.

Teacher–Teacher

Building strong relationships between teachers will influence the well-being of teachers and, in turn, that of students. Treating other teachers in ways that make them feel good about themselves will create a more positive environment for everyone. The teachers on staff need to be able to act in kindness and consideration of one another. They need to accept one another's limitations and to celebrate what each teacher brings to the staff. With each action, you have the power to make other teachers feel good about themselves. Actions or ways of responding influence the way your staff members feel about themselves and about you.

A fellow teacher organizes a playday at your school. You would have done it completely differently. What action do you take? Does it build positive relationships?
- Tell her what she did well.
  Yes: Makes the person feel great and lets her know what she should do again.
- Say nothing. She did her best and took on a huge task.
  No: The person might feel that she did a lot of work that no one noticed.
- Tell her what she should have done differently.
  No: This increases stress, since there is nothing she can do and, in turn, fix it.
- Take notes in your head of things that could be done differently and make a list for next year's playday committee.
  Yes: Without causing stress and creating negativity, you set up the next event for more success.

Teacher–Class

The teacher's treatment of the whole class will affect the level of stress in the classroom and the way in which everyone acts toward themselves and others. You must be able to examine how you manage a whole classroom. What classroom management strategies are you using? What teaching strategies are you using to deliver your program. Is the classroom run in an authoritarian, exploratory, or permissive way? How do you gain classroom control? How do your actions influence the way your students treat one another?

> Your students are not working well and are not on task. What do you do? Does it build positive relationships?
> - Yell at them and tell them that they need to work or you will make them stay after school.
>   No: You are treating children in a way that you likely tell them not to treat others.
> - You indicate to them that they have not accomplished enough work up until now. You create a short but clear task list that they must complete before you take a break as a class.
>   Yes: By establishing a clear *first/then* situation, you are setting up your students for success.
> - You assess the situation and realize that they are not regulated and, unless you switch the activity, the rest of the period will go badly. You take a break and resume the task at a later time.
>   Yes: You are assessing the capacity of your students and adapting your needs to meet theirs.

Teacher–Student

It is important to monitor and control your responses to the challenging student; i.e., the student who does not follow the classroom codes of conduct, who disrupts learning, and who sometimes hurts other children. The way teachers manage the behavior of an individual student sets the tone for how the whole class will interact with this student.

> Your whole class is actively engaged, but one student keeps disrupting and making annoying sounds. How do you handle the student? Does it build positive relationships?
> - You indicate that you need his help in the hallway and you speak with him privately in the hall.
>   Yes: You are showing him that you are there to help him, but that you will do it in a supportive and private way.
> - You grumble to him that he is disturbing the class.
>   No: You are treating him unkindly, in a way that does not support a positive classroom environment.
> - You tell another student to tell him that his behavior is bothering her.
>   No: Without guidance and support, this interaction is likely to be unkind and unnecessarily rough.

Student Relationships

Teachers must be able to examine how they facilitate both big and small interactions between each layer of student relationships; moreover, teachers must understand that each of those interactions influences the way each student in the classroom thinks and feels.

Student–Self

Every individual has a different way of viewing, interpreting, and perceiving themselves and their actions in the world. As a teacher, you must be aware of each student's self-perception and the tendencies of their personal thoughts and feelings. You can support your students in recognizing their tendencies toward positive or negative thinking, and in examining their interpretations and the implications of those interpretations for their daily successes and struggles.

> During a basketball unit in gym class, you witness a student's whole body language change. At the beginning of the game, she appeared content, but as she misses baskets her shoulders slouch, her smile fades, and she slows down her movements. You observe her grumbling to herself. You hear her say, "I am such a loser. I am the worst athlete ever. I can't do anything." What action do you take? Does it build positive relationships?
> - Cheer her on as she goes past you.
>   No: This is positive and encouraging, but it does not have much substance. It is general encouragement and will likely not alter the way she thinks and feels.
> - Do nothing. This student always does this, but then she gets over it.
>   No: You have witnessed a student scold herself and you have not taken a step to support her.
> - Use positive self-talk (see page 23) with her to try to redirect her thinking. "Focus on something positive. Focus on one thing you have done well. I saw you block Rita's shot. That was positive. There are some positive things happening today; it is great to see them, too."
>   Yes: The benefit of positive self-talk is that it directs a child's thinking, but does not require the child to do anything active. The student might or might not take in what you have said today, but the positive self-talk is heard by the student and often applied over time.

Student–Student

Examine how you facilitate interaction between students. Students can be taught to support each other. Or they can be left to problem-solve on their own, without guidance and intervention, which often results in patterns of social behavior between children that are not fair and healthy. Consider that your treatment of negative behaviors might indicate that these behaviors are permissible.

> A student rolls his eyes at another student. What action do you take? Does it build positive relationships?
> - Do nothing; it was not physical interaction.
>   No: You are turning a blind eye to an act of meanness. If we respond to only significant acts of bullying, we miss opportunities to establish the ways we should treat one another and the processes by which we can make amends for social unkindness.

- Approach the situation slowly and join in. Smile at both students, an outward expression of being positive and relaxed. Ask them if they are remembering to use their positive interaction skills and are supporting each other. Let them know that it can be hard to remember all the kind and gentle ways to treat a friend; e.g., looking at them while they are speaking, nodding in agreement as often as you can, resisting rolling your eyes or contradicting them.
Yes: You manage to address an issue in a unobtrusive way. You did not attack or place anyone on the spot, but you reviewed rules and engaged in the process.

Student–Class

Examine how you facilitate the interaction between one student and the rest. A single student has the power to set the tone and dynamic of the whole class. Teachers play a vital role in monitoring and overseeing that relationship.

A student in the class is consistently directing and controlling the other students. He seems to glare at students until they do things for him. Or he cries until fellow students do what he wants. He can simply walk into a classroom and the other students look at him to get his approval for what they can and can't do. You observe that he whispers to others and they change their behavior. What action do you take? Does it build positive relationships?
- Tell the student to stop telling others what to do.
  No: The negative comment does not explain to him what he is doing and how to act differently.
- Consistently direct the student to consider the thoughts and feelings of other students in the class.
  Yes: This will be a long process, but it will help the student begin to consider the thoughts, feelings, and needs of others.
- Slowly approach a situation in which he is telling other students what to do; without corrections, engage with him and gently question him about what is happening.
  Yes: This approach forces the student to put words to his actions, and begins a non-defensive dialogue.

Class–Student

Examine how you facilitate the interaction between the whole class (or a group of children) and one student. A class can act together as a group, supporting and following a child, neglecting and isolating another.

Your whole class struggles with one student. You know yourself how difficult this student is; it is often she who creates the problems and begins the antagonism. However, the whole class has come together against her. What action do you take? Does it build positive relationships?
- You ignore the issue. Maybe she will finally learn.
  No: Allowing students to gang up against one child condones bullying in your classroom.

- Tell all students that their behavior is unacceptable and that they had better be nice to the girl, because she has problems.
  No: You are pushing an issue without supporting your students through it. This will leave more children upset.
- Take up a more active presence in the classroom and sit with the girl more often during group work.
  Yes: By being actively involved in settling conflicts, you can prompt students to speak softly to each other and ensure they are listening to their peers

For all the examples in this chapter, teachers will have different strategies to handle adverse situations: some active, some passive. Some strategies result in positive outcomes for self and other, while others in negative outcomes for self and other. As we begin to better understand positive and negative ways of acting, we can group these actions into different processes.

2

Giving Positive Response

As teachers, we have power to create the environment in which we work and interact with our students. This power does not take the form of posters on the wall or words of advice to our students, but is built through our daily interactions with our students, situation by situation. The way we act in any given moment is our most effective tool. A positive response, delivered in a controlled, thoughtful, deliberate manner, with a teaching purpose and intent behind the action, models what we teach children and guides them through challenging moments.

A positive response can be easy when things are going well, when we feel healthy and regulated, and when students are engaged in learning and following routines. But when children struggle, we often act in one of two ways: we ignore the underlying issue and leave them to learn on their own, or we react to their behavior and reprimand. This response cycle, to ignore and/or criticize harshly, fails these children and causes them internal confusion because our own behavior differs from what we tell them about behavior and its consequences.

We need to understand how to support children's growth and development. We need to create and foster interactions that enhance relationships with self and other, that result in a positive classroom climate. We need to understand how to respond in specific situations to naturally attain social-emotional well-being and decrease the negativity and stress children are exposed to. So what response to student behavior will do this?

Acting on Student Behavior

As we saw in the last chapter, there are multiple layers to the relationships in each class. They present many different choices for a teacher to make quickly, in hard situations, so a class can move forward in a positive way and students feel supported. If this is hard on teachers, the same challenge exists for all students in the classroom. It is hard for children to determine how they should interact in certain situations, based only on their own ideas and background, their interpretation and management. We need to have systems in place to teach these children repeated behavior strategies that will work throughout their lives.

> When Xander complains that Malcolm does not stop tapping him, he is given different advice from each adult in his life. His parents tell him to ask Malcolm to stop. One teacher tells Xander to focus and stay on task; another tells him to ignore Malcolm; Xander is told to move by a third. Finally, a last teacher tells Malcolm to stop bugging Xander and disciplines him. As long as the same problem is handled in different ways, it is challenging for Xander to sort out

> what he should actually do to get Malcolm to stop. In the end, it creates in Xander a reliance upon a teacher to intervene in the situation, since he is unsure which approach any particular teacher prefers. However, if we teach and support the children, consistently giving them the same advice and help, both Xander and Malcolm will learn the social-emotional skills to deal with this situation and others.

How do we consistently support our students? We establish problem-solving as a schoolwide process, first for the teachers themselves and then for students. If schools provide guiding principles for approaching problems, they can address the problems instead of merely the symptoms of each disagreement; for example, it is better to regulate, engage, and support students through relationship-building processes than to address an issue like bullying in isolation. With guiding principles in place, teachers do not need to determine how to handle a problem and how they should be reacting each time. The procedure will guide them through facilitating the interaction between children, who are themselves guided by the same principles. The procedure is based on the goal of building relationships and strengthening a positive community.

There are three actions we can take in the face of challenging behaviors of students. We can

- Ignore: display a lack of reaction to the behavior or situation
- React: act quickly with emotion, with the goal of solving the problem immediately
- Respond: use the moment as a learning opportunity to elicit positive interaction through regulation, engagement, and support

Ignore

Ignoring the situation is a passive approach. If you do not respond to social moments, your students will miss many learning opportunities. Just as we go out of our way to teach curriculum basics, we need to go out of our way to guide children to engage positively with others. Without our intervention, building healthy relationships becomes more of a challenge, and this will ultimately have a negative affect on our students' mental health and well-being. Your ignoring of behaviors and situations can leave children feeling unsupported, unheard, and unhelped.

React

A reactionary approach is often a negative one. If your behavior models treating others in a way that is opposite to how we tell students to treat each other, it leaves students confused and stressed. Being attacked, scolded, or lectured leaves children perplexed and unsure. It makes them defensive and will result in them pushing back, closing themselves off from the experience of being shown and taught. A less extreme example of reacting is the teacher who comes in quickly and dominates the situation in order to solve the problem. The teacher should not be the leader or problem-solver, but the facilitator of interactions between all individuals in the class.

Respond

Unlike the negative approach of reacting to improve a single behavior or situation, responding is a positive approach that takes into consideration ourselves, the student, and all relationships. If we go out of our way to seek opportunities to support ourselves and others, then we are attempting to improve our social-emotional well-being through positive relationships and a positive climate. Instead of reacting, we must monitor our responses and act only once we know our response is part of a positive process. By responding in a more controlled and deliberate manner, we are problem-solving and reducing stress for teachers and students on a larger scale.

Leah is in Grade 6. She struggles with depression.

Leah comes into the classroom and slouches at her desk. She is disengaged and lacks interest. She rarely contributes or engages in discussions, unless it is to complain about something or someone, or to question the need to do what she has been asked to do. She has met with a few different social workers; her teacher from the preceding year says that she spent a lot of time with her, chatting about what was upsetting her and what made her feel sad, but that it never got anywhere.

Ignore
You continue to engage with Leah and to teach her as best you can, but you do not get sidetracked by her complaining or her questions.

React
You tell Leah that part of being a contributing member of society is to pretend to be a part of the group and to be engaged in the activities, whether she likes them or not. Even if she feels tired on the inside, you see her job as a student as being positive and getting involved. Tell her that if she fakes it and tries to look like she is happy, she will likely begin to feel happy.

Respond
Understand that Leah's natural tendency is to observe and notice negatives more than positives in her environment. To help Leah, gradually examine her propensity for negative experiences and reactions, and consistently support her in more positively appreciating her environment and experience.

The Positive Response Process

For all teaching, we work side-by-side with students to guide them through the process of learning. It begins when we set up a task up so that the child is working in his/her zone of proximal development; i.e., just above the student's level of proficiency. We support the child as he/she begins the task, moves through it, and completes it. Throughout this process, we are assessing and looking for times to pull back, times to step in, and times when we need to provide some form of prompt or guidance to support the process.

We can apply this process when a child is experiencing social-emotional struggles as well. Each time a student experiences stress from a trigger, we can be there to assist him/her in self-assessment, to create a plan of action, to calm him/her and the environment, to demonstrate understanding, and to guide the student through a task that targets the development of essential social-emotional character traits.

We want to engage in a process that builds relationships, allows teachers to focus on themselves, and allows them to teach students the necessary calming and mental-health strategies. A response is a deliberately positive approach. It considers the bigger picture and has relationship development, social-emotional skills, and character traits at its base. It supports a child's learning through his/her strengths and weaknesses alike. Being perfect or the best at something is not a prerequisite for a teacher's guidance through a positive response process—all types of mistakes are supported.

The Positive Response Process has five steps:

1. Give Feedback: Self-assess and set new goals to drive the process
2. Set Goals: Plan
3. Regulate: Use calming strategies
4. Engage: Be available, attend; show compassion, understanding
5. Support: Guide; do not direct, solve, tell, or lead

> The point is not to always eliminate triggers from a child's environment. Schools have rules, routines, and expectations, and so does the real world. Removing all things that upset a child will not help that child develop the skills needed to face those challenges.

Give Feedback

Children need to have a good sense of their social-emotional abilities. But students often receive feedback at the end of a process and then move on to the next task, which can leave them unable to apply their learning again to the same, or a similar, challenge. They identify their strengths and challenges and then move on to something new, without connecting the feedback to strategies for working through the task. This makes the mastery of any activity or skill challenging. We want feedback on a previous activity or attempt to drive all goal-setting and criteria in the future in an appropriate way. Children should be able to ask themselves:
- *What worked and what didn't?*
- *How am I doing?*
- *What do I need to work on?*
- *What is my challenge and what can I do to mitigate it?*
- *What did I do well yesterday and how can I apply that again today?*
- *Where did I struggle and what will I do in order to prevent the same pitfalls?*

> Feedback is nothing but negative criticism if the student cannot do anything at the point at which the feedback is given.

Set Goals

We need to assist children in their goal-setting in a considerate and manageable manner. Children need a clear understanding of the goal and it needs to be attainable. Children use feedback to concentrate on the steps, skills, and criteria they will need to get through their next task or skill development. An important first step in goal-setting is verbalizing the process:
- identifying the strategy they would like to practice
- detailing the first steps they will take
- explaining to others what help they could use during challenging moments

> If we begin with feedback and setting goals, we have already developed the process before we begin.

Goal-Setting Activity

Creating a Positive Scale engages students in exploring what experiences, activities, actions, or material possessions make them happy. It is important for students not only to be able to identify the positives in their lives, but also to be able to rate these experiences, to distinguish between the things in life that truly make

The Positive Response Process 21

them happy and the things they might want desperately but will not bring them as much happiness.

1. Have students list what makes them happy.
2. Students put the list items in order of how happy the experiences make them.
3. Students chart experiences on a numbered line graph to show a scale of positive experiences.

The point of charting positive experiences is that, by visually arranging their perception of positive experiences, students can see them and reflect on them. They might also come to make changes to their charts as they begin to understand how experiences can change in importance.

It is important, however, to not make judgment or suggestions as you guide students through this activity. In the sample Positive Scale shown here, the student lists a Mars bar as more positive than playing soccer with her father. The teacher scribing for the student did not comment or suggest; she did not want to question the student's veracity or perception. Over time, we want to slowly assist students in understanding which rewards are meaningful and sustain us.

SAMPLE POSITIVE SCALE

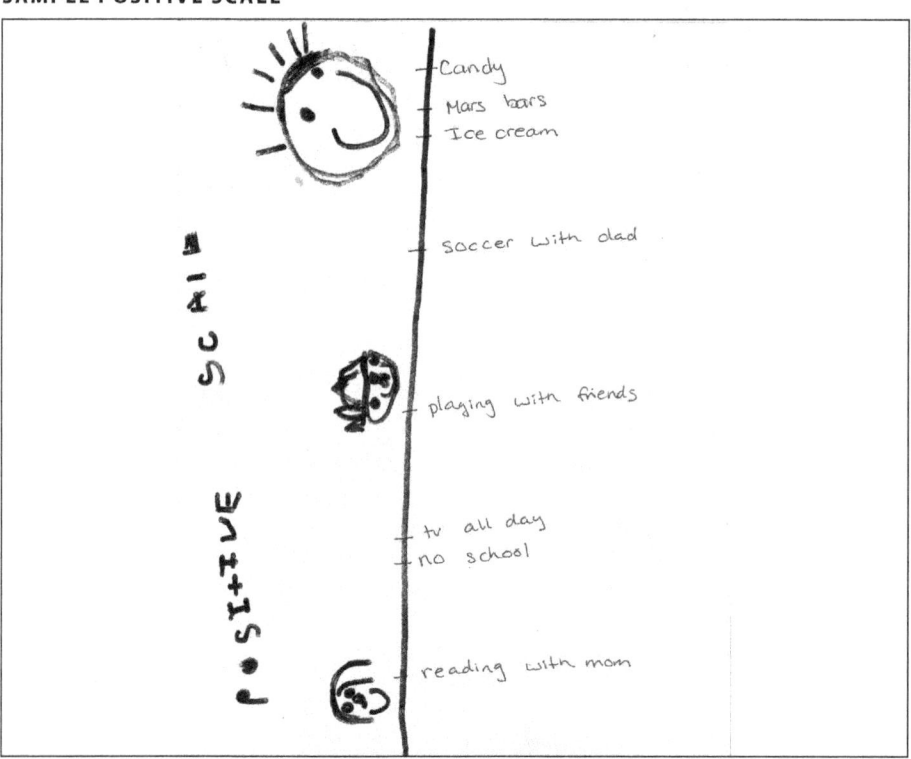

Regulate

To be regulated is to be in a calm state, emotionally and physically. If teacher and student are in the Flight, Flight, or Freeze state, stress reduction is impossible. To help children self-calm, we must first ensure that we, ourselves, are calm and regulated, that we are responding to them in a thoughtful and deliberate manner. We, and only we, are responsible for our own regulation and state of calm. No one else is looking out for it.

Too often, we calm students by solving their problems for them. Our aim in the Positive Response Process is to calm them so that they can solve their problems themselves.

As teachers, we have an important role in teaching children to self-calm. We must

- stabilize the environment and create regulation for students by supporting them through self-calming techniques, without the expectation that they know how to do them independently
- understand that it will take a long time for all and a very long time for others
- slow the pace of interactions and draw our attention to a child's physical and emotional body language as we interact and engage with them. If our movements and those of the students are rushed and unstructured, then the child will be deregulated.
- take time to help students practice self-calming strategies, to increase their mental well-being and make them ready to learn
- make simplifications in activities and life as external ways to assist in students' regulation

Your guiding principle should be to calm students first, before supporting them through problem-solving. The problem-solving process happens much faster when children are calm.

Engage

The purpose of engagement is to provide positive support. It can be nonverbal or verbal, but it is based in positivity.

The Positive Response Process requires us to be responsive and emotionally available to our students:

- to react thoughtfully to their behavior
- to notice their state of regulation, physiologically and emotionally
- to be attuned to their needs, not our own needs or the needs of the task
- to respond to their emotional reactions and physiological responses
- to guide them through their struggles, not problem-solve for them

Using Positive Self-Talk

Throughout this book, you will find prompts that link to the life skills and fundamental concepts you are teaching students. Use positive self-talk daily in the moment with your students to link their negative struggles to the positive actions and underlying character traits that can help see them through. Positive self-talk prompts can be put on the announcements or made into posters, but they are most effective when they are repeatedly linked to an action a student can take in a recognizable situation. Place written messages of positive self-talk around the room for students to use, and use them yourself every time you struggle with stress.

Support

Supporting involves helping a student in the application of social-emotional goals in the moment. When students are under stress, we can assist them in their performance of a skill-building activity or attempts at a social-emotional strategy by

- prompting them to use their preferred strategies
- cuing them to the first step in their process
- using positive self-talk
- using nonverbal reminders
- modeling effective techniques
- facilitating peer dialogue and communication so students support each other

Using the example of Leah (page 20), the Positive Response Process might look like this.

Give Feedback

If you see Leah engaging in a positive way with a friend, or even smiling, take the opportunity to describe to her in detail what she looks like and the positive effect it has; for example, "I saw you chatting with Riley. It looked like you were having a good time together. You appeared confident and happy. You had a smile from ear to ear while you were talking to him. It looked fun." Use descriptive feedback of an event to tie in what Leah might be overlooking in her daily life; for example, "Sometimes we forget these positive experiences during the day and only remember the hard parts. When you think back about today, do you think you will remember this friendly interaction?"

Set Goals

Set a simple plan with Leah to "catch" two positive experiences a day and write them down. She can record them in a special notebook that you provide or on a list that goes up in the classroom for all the students to add to. Once you have a list of things that Leah has listed as positives, help her rate them by creating a Positive Scale (see page 22). Initially, Leah might list that the cookie in her lunch is a 9 and the fact that her mom and dad give her hugs is a 4. Do not rush to correct this or to have her change her placement of them. This is part of the exploration process that we want children to learn.

Regulate

When Leah begins to complain about events of the day, calm yourself before speaking with her. Take one step back, close your eyes, and/or take a breath. Take one more breath while you decide how you want to approach her and what you will say. Cue Leah to model your actions: to take her own step back, close her eyes, and take a breath before you begin to speak with each other.

Engage

Smile at Leah and relax your body. Attempt to send your first message through positive body language. Walk over slowly and sit down beside her with a smile, before using any words. Show that you hear her. Your first words to her should not be why she is wrong or what she should be thinking or feeling. First show understanding and demonstrate that you are on her side; for example, "That does look frustrating. The answer is not obvious." Then pause before trying to determine five active steps to take.

Support

Leah might not yet be ready to identify two positive things in the situation or to apply the goals she has set for herself in the moment. Supporting Leah might take the form of modeling the positive self-talk strategies you hope she will learn in time, without expecting her to say anything; for example, "The good thing about this situation is that we have lots of time to figure out the problem and there are helpful friends in the classroom who can brainstorm with us." This positive self-talk does not tell Leah what to do or how to feel, but empathizes with her and provides a positive way of looking at the situation.

Social-Emotional Character Traits

Positive relationships with self and others come more naturally to some children than to others. Some children seem to naturally navigate and manage the stressors that pop up each day, while others are significantly affected by stresses, letting them trigger a negative cycle that depletes their energy and resources and those of the people around them. Students and teachers who are better able to cope with stress not only are less sensitive to stress itself, but also possess a cluster of social-emotional traits that lie behind their successful stress management.

It is important to examine the basic character traits that allow some people to function well through school and life, and that result in academic, social, and emotional well-being. In schools, we often look at these traits in terms of how they affect academic and life success. We talk about the importance of *self-control*, *obedience*, and *compassion* as traits essential to building strong, caring communities and helping learners. Popular character trait terms might include *responsibility*, *optimism*, *perseverance*, *zest*, *empathy*, *self-regulation*, and *respect*. But character education goes beyond the words for the character traits. The specific moments when a teacher links a child's awareness of his/her actions to a positive outcome in the class are at the heart of successful character-building. For example, catch a student in an act of perseverance and say, "I saw that you were struggling to get your knapsack off the hook. It was really high up and you looked defeated. But you kept trying. You kept pushing yourself and you kept attempting to get it off the hook yourself. Still, it was hard for you. I wondered if you were going to give up. Do you know if you felt like giving up, or if you knew that you would keep trying? Anyway, then you used a book to push your backpack over the hook. I thought it was a brilliant idea. But I was most impressed by how hard you kept trying."

Social-emotional character traits influence the way we interact with our environment and the way we perceive events in our lives. These traits can become entrenched into the way we think and feel about ourselves and others. We need to learn how to teach these traits to all students, not just explaining them as part of a social-emotional curriculum, but also teaching them as a process that develops them in students, day in and day out.

This book will examine specific social-emotional character traits instrumental to the ability to manage stress. These traits help students and teachers face stress in schools and manage it, not by simply coping with it (which can involve avoiding stress or engaging in other dysfunctional behaviors), but by being able to identify stress, decrease its pressure, and practice applying strategies that deal with it.

Social-emotional character traits are ways of behaving, thinking, and feeling. They are often based on the situation or activity at hand, as well as how the individual feels on that day; for example, a child who has strong social-emotional skills during math class, because he/she loves math and is good at it, might not have strong social-emotional skills during gym class, because he/she does not love sports and struggles with physical activities. Recognizing that social-emotional skills are not static is crucial when teaching them. We want to avoid telling a child that he/she is amazing at something or is strong in a particular social-emotional skill, because the next day we might not observe the same behavior, thinking, and feeling being applied to another situation. Instead, we want to focus on the positive actions, thinking, and behavior that a student is using in

> When supporting academic character traits, consult your school board's character education program and, where possible, follow it. The success of these programs comes from common language and a repetitive message used year after year by different teachers.

the moment and, where possible, label it as a particular skill. We want to tie the action, thinking, or feeling to the student's ability to navigate a challenge.

We can divide key social-emotional character traits that are instrumental to stress management into three categories: awareness, acceptance, and ability to manage stress.

Awareness

Knowledge is the first step in the process of stress-management, because knowledge allows students to give themselves feedback and set goals. Awareness is key to stress-management because we need to be able to know and identify the causes of stress and the personal ways in which we and those around us react to it. Those who know their own behavior, thinking, and feeling tendencies, and who are able to identify the behavior, thinking, and feeling tendencies of others, are better able to understand each situation at hand.

Acceptance

Acceptance functions to decrease pressure and expectation of perfection. Students need to be able to identify challenges to themselves or others, to understand that challenges are okay and that things need to be worked on. Acceptance can prevent them getting stuck or breaking down, and can avoid a negative cycle of emotions toward self (guilt, shame, embarrassment) or others (blame, disappointment, anger). Tolerance of challenges, seeing them as problems to be solved, keeps the student from escalating up the stress curve into further dysregulation.

Ability to Manage Stress

Our ability to apply what we have learned in the moment under stress allows for successful stress-management. Students can know and understand their stresses, but if they are not motivated or able to use strategies in times of stress, to try difficult and new techniques, and to apply that learning, they will not be able to reduce their stress once they face it. A lack of motivation does not imply that a student is lazy or lethargic. He/she might not be motivated enough to push through because there is someone else willing to come in and help, or because he/she does not see the end goal as worth the effort. Finding the right motivators is essential to supporting students in taking steps to tackle challenges. Students who can tackle setbacks, obstacles, and hard moments are those who are motivated and able to push through a challenging task and to try again, even if they were previously unsuccessful.

3

Awareness

Awareness is an essential social-emotional trait that contributes to our ability to manage stress because it begins the process of goal-setting. If we learn what causes stress and identify our personal sensitivities and those of the people around us, we will be able to problem-solve and plan to alter the way we act, think, and feel. In this chapter, we will examine awareness of

- our strengths
- our challenges
- the strengths and challenges of others
- stress triggers
- the impact of stress on the body
- the impact of stress on behavior
- the impact of stress on thinking
- the impact of stress on feelings

Of Strengths

Objective: To develop a complete understanding of positive character traits and sense of self in order to understand the dynamics we bring to our relationships with self and others.

> Jason is in Grade 4. He struggles in school.
> Jason has always been a slow reader and finds math confusing. He loves athletics, but is not particularly strong in any sport. Jason has been looking a little sad lately, and he seems out of sorts. It appears that he is becoming aware of his academic difficulties. You realize that Jason is not aware of his strengths: his strong character and the valuable role he plays in class as a peacekeeper and friend. Jason is always an excellent partner, even when grouped with children who become easily upset or argue. He always manages to set order to a dysfunctional group. It is not completely clear if he knows about this ability of his and that he does it on purpose. His natural tendency to speak slowly and in a soft voice somehow calms the other students. He is always positive and he listens well to the ideas of the other students, so that they feel like they were heard in the group.
>
> *Ignore*
> You tell Jason he is a great leader and that he has tremendous strengths. This is obviously a positive statement, but its generality does not provide Jason with information he can use to understand why he is a leader.

> *React*
> You tell the other students in the class that they should be leaders like Jason.
>
> *Response*
> Try to catch Jason doing something well once a day. Break down his positive actions and link them to the positive social-emotional character traits that contribute to group success; for example, connect his listening to and supporting of his peers during group work to his leadership and attentive character.

It is necessary for students to understand the social-emotional character traits they possess that result in successful interactions with others and that allow them to confidently approach and function in situations.

The character trait of awareness of personal strengths provides students with the knowledge of their dynamics with themselves and with those around them. Through this knowledge, students are better able to understand the positive attributes they bring to a situation, what they can bring to their relationships, and how this can affect their classroom as a whole. Teachers can provide consistent opportunities for students to directly examine their strengths and develop a strong sense of self.

Teachers can support students by knowing them. Students can support themselves by knowing themselves.

You can emphasize the personal strengths that lead students to succeed in specific areas and the personal strengths that will support them socially and emotionally. Increase their awareness of the social and interpersonal strengths that they use during daily interactions. Provide opportunities for students to know themselves. They can explore personal goals, feelings, thinking, relationships, and actions in search of their identity. Students are more reflective of situations and relationships if they know what works well in their lives.

What is required is a deep knowledge of a student's strengths, an understanding that goes beyond general descriptions. Most students would be able to summarize what they are good at doing; for example, a student might say, "I am good in school" or "I am great in sports." These are valid accomplishments, but they are goals and successes external to the student. We want to focus on the social-emotional character strengths that foster a child's ongoing development and the qualities that lead to inner success. The development of these qualities will optimize a child's life skills and lead to a strong and healthy student. We want to support students in increasing their self-awareness, not simply in terms of what they are good at doing, but also in terms of who they are. This process does not arise out of general positive statements, such as "I am nice." A general statement does not let a student recognize the qualities he or she possesses that result in being nice to others. It also leads to feelings of guilt when the student acts in ways that he/she knows know do not correspond with the positive self-identification.

A focus on social-emotional character traits values the process over the product.

True awareness of one's strengths comes from consistent goal-setting and self-reflection within tasks. Every interaction, conflict, and challenge can be seen as an opportunity for reflection about the positive contributions that facilitate the individual in beginning, persisting, and completing a task. This self-reflection is not about the quality of the completion of the task; i.e., "I did a wonderful job writing a perfect book report." It focuses on the qualities that gave the student the motivation to start a daunting task or to persevere when the task seemed impossible. The qualities that allowed a child to compromise when he/she did not want to or, to adapt to the needs of others, are the strengths that will decrease challenging moments in the child's life, and that, in turn, will decrease stress.

Awareness-Building Activity

Create charts with students to examine the difference between the qualities of success in terms that a student can understand. For every ability, there are different social-emotional skills that could be responsible for assisting a child in its success.

SAMPLE SOCIAL-EMOTIONAL TRAIT CHART

Ability	Actions	Social-Emotional Character Trait
Great in math	Continuing to problem-solve and try alternative scenarios even when the work appears overwhelming	Perseverance
Talented dancer	Going to classes four days a week	Responsibility
Successful leader and negotiator	Listening to the ideas of a group and supporting them all so that they believe they are heard and understood	Cooperation
Good friend	Attending to others as they express their thoughts and feelings	Empathy

As we examine the chart, it becomes clear that telling students they are good friends or empathetic does not explain why they are. We want to explain to children the actions that make them good friends or empathetic; for example, "You were a great friend when John was upset. You looked at him, nodded to show understanding, and repeated what he said to show that you heard him. These actions are the substance of being a good friend."

> ### Relationship: Student–Class
>
> Students need to understand that positive social-emotional character traits are the basis of what allow them to have a positive influence on themselves and on others. We can consistently remind our students that our goal is to have a positive influence on ourselves and others. You can make a chart with your class to highlight the positive actions students can take that have positive effects.
>
> **SAMPLE POSITIVE ACTION CHART**
>
> | Positive Action that Makes a Group Work Well | Positive Influence on the Group |
> |---|---|
> | Speak slowly with your friends. | Everyone's energy seems calmer. |
> | Use a soft voice. | Keeps other people's voices down. |
> | Smile and look happy. | Everyone else feels happier. |
> | Turn and look at your friends. | Makes people feel included. |

| Nod in agreement with what people say. | People feel great because their ideas are recognized. |
| Restate what the person said. | People think they are being heard. |

The Positive Response Process

Give Feedback

If you notice that recess has been going much better lately—less conflict, more successful working and playing together—take the opportunity to examine this success. Instead of saying, "Great work, everyone. Recess is going a lot better," as students come in from recess, take ten minutes before recess to celebrate successful recesses and to link the success to social-emotional character traits and skills.

SAMPLE POSITIVE FEEDBACK CHART

Why Recess Has Been Better	Actions	Social-emotional Character Trait
Less fighting	Walking away and taking a break	Self-control
More sharing	Thinking about how our friends feel	Empathy
Group games	Being flexible about what games we want	Cooperation

> **Relationship: Teacher–Student**
>
> My friend Ilaria, who runs the B.E.N. Schoolhouse in Toronto, marks her students' successes (cleaning up their lunch without being asked, not interrupting, removing themselves when they think they might make a bad choice) by giving them a painted stone. The students keep the stones and value them as special gifts from their attentive teacher. Ilaria says, "Make sure the students know that you believe it is worth taking the time to notice and celebrate their achievements, specifically the less-obvious ones."

Set Goals

Use your students' self-reflections to reinforce their strengths and their understanding of the skills behind their strengths. Pick one character trait a month and allow each student to come up with a few tangible ways to achieve that goal. For example, if the character trait for your classroom is *kindness*, tangible ways for each student to be kind would be to smile at five classmates each day, to ask at least one student a day how he/she is feeling, and to try to hold the door open for the person behind him/her every time they go through doors.

Regulate

Capitalize on your students' strengths and interests by using a social-emotional skill as an effective tool for something that the student finds challenging. For

---

You do not need to give a reward or make a large event to celebrate successes with students. It is important to acknowledge small successes as often as possible, even if it is just making note of them, writing them on the board, or giving a group high-five.

example, examine the interests of a student who is quick to lose his temper and often gets into trouble. Find an activity he enjoys and involve it in his self-calming process: if the student loves music, his self-calming strategy could include singing a song in his head.

Engage

Use your students' self-assessments to guide their behavior. Once you are aware of the abilities and strengths a student sees in him/herself and considers important, attend to that behavior and expand on it as much as you can. This is not just about praising the students who are on task, doing what all students should be doing; it is about focusing on what students are proud of in themselves. For example, if a student writes in her assessment that she is proud of herself because she is nice, capitalize on the statement and expand on it. Catch her in the act of being kind to another child and detail the actions that make it kind: "Thank you for lining up right away. You wrote in your self-reflection that you are *kind*. This is a great example of your kindness. You do not want members of your classroom to have to wait for you, so you quickly gathered your belongings and got right into line. It is kind to think about the needs of others. Thanks." This strategy expands on a general idea of the student's and ties it positively into the actions of the day.

Support

Use a self-reflection sheet (see page 32 for a template) directly after an activity, encouraging students to examine their behavior and to link it to a positive group experience. You do not need to have pre-made sheets; you can write in the student's notebook and have the student comment, or students can write in their own notebooks.

SAMPLE CHECKLIST

Self-Reflection Checklist

Name: _____ Date: _____

Topic: _____

I explained my ideas ☐ calmly.
 ☐ softly.
 ☐ patiently.
 ☐ other: _____.

I used positive body language:
☐ I smiled.
☐ I nodded my head.
☐ I turned my body toward my partner.
☐ I monitored my face; i.e., I did not roll my eyes or glare.
☐ Other: _____.

☐ I let my partner have a turn talking.
☐ I listened to my partner's ideas.
☐ I tried to be open to my partner's ideas.
☐ I did not agree with my partner on everything, but I made sure we compromised.

We followed my ideas about

_____

_____

_____

We followed his/her ideas about

_____

_____

_____

Pembroke Publishers ©2014 *Stop the Stress in Schools* by Joey Mandel ISBN 978-1-55138-298-2

Of Challenges

Objective: To be self-reflective and examine our struggles in order to understand the dynamics they bring to our relationships with self and other.

Jerry is in Grade 2

Jerry is rather strong academically and has many interests. He is always on the go and actively wants to join in. But during many interactions he becomes upset. He can always be heard yelling at his friends and telling them what to do. Within a few minutes, he comes running up to complain about someone. He yells that they are unfair or that it is his turn. He argues that they did something against him or to him.

Ignore

You become good at solving Jerry's problems for him. You are quickly able to calm him down by telling the other children to stop or by telling Jerry to play somewhere else.

React

You tell Jerry that his complaining is a challenge of his and that he needs to learn to deal with others better.

Response

Assist Jerry in understanding the aspects of his personality that make it hard for him when he plays with others. Partner Jerry with a peer who is strong in the social-emotional character qualities in which Jerry is weak, a peer who is flexible and can see another person's perspective. Examine the positive aspects of the peer's qualities (see page 29). Discuss the strengths the peer possesses that help him/her successfully deal with similar problems. Do this in a subtle way, without direct comparison; i.e., do not compare Jerry with the peer, or tell Jerry that he should be more like his partner.

Supporting Jerry to understand the qualities he could work on is a long process. Do not rush this and do not go into this activity thinking that Jerry's challenges will be solved quickly.

We support children through the difficult process of self-examination and awareness of their own struggles as a necessary first step in developing their ability to take ownership of the dynamic of their relationships with themselves and others. A true awareness of how a student views the world, interacts in it, and interacts with him/herself and others will allow for better understanding of life successes and challenges that he/she will face over time.

Use an open process of awareness to examine how we interact and share space with others during each social contact. This examination should not focus on what students do badly, such as academic work or activities. It should not be a list of what they do wrong and need to stop doing. Negative self-awareness can lead to extreme anxiety that debilitates children. Those who excessively self-monitor and seek perfectionism will create huge pressures on themselves and will experience high anxiety each time they catch themselves doing something they believe they need to fix.

Positive Self-Talk: *The more I know about myself, the more I will understand my relationships with others.*

Students can seek a greater understanding of the problem underlying their struggles and how they might be influencing or contributing to it. They begin with short and simple reflections, examining the situations they find challenging and difficult. Be prepared to assist students in their scrutiny of their own behavior, core beliefs, and assumptions. Support them in examining the thinking and feeling they bring to situations that hold them back as learners or cause them challenges.

The self-reflection loses its value if it is not tied closely to an activity or interaction. Handing out general worksheets to all students at the same time and asking them to list their strengths and challenges does not assist in the self-discovery process in the moment; it links the negative outcome of a situation to an aspect of the child's behavior. Without judgment or punishment, we want to provide opportunities for self-reflection that will allow a child to examine his/her contribution to a situation that resulted in conflict or misinterpretation. The student could be asked to self-reflect on what occurred in the group dynamic that created a large problem out of a small problem.

Awareness-Building Activity

Just as with positive social-emotional character traits, support students in examining their actions and the impact of those actions in situations that turn negative. Create charts with students that examine the actions behind the descriptive terms they hear on the playground or think about themselves or others. Explain to them that rarely does a person display just one character trait. We all engage in behaviors that are positive and could be defined by a positive character trait; while other times, when we are under stress or during an activity that we are not as good at, we engage in behavior or actions that exhibit negative social-emotional characteristics. The negative characteristics do not define the type of person we are. A general term does not need to be used to describe who a person is.

Relationship: Student–Self

When children engage in unhealthy behavior, they might define themselves as negative because of that action. For example, if one child has said unkind things to another child, he/she might come to the conclusion, "I am mean." Emphasize to children that a single action does not make them "mean"; it is simply that they engaged in actions that had a negative impact on themselves and others.

SAMPLE CHALLENGE CHART

Challenge or Struggle	Actions	Social-Emotional Character Trait
Not a good friend	• Yelling at friends when under stress • Saying things out loud that he/she should keep inside his/her head	Meanness, unkindness

Controlling and bossy	• Not being able to accept the ideas of others • Not being able to change his/her mind in mid-course • Getting stuck on a way of doing things	Rigidity, inflexibility
Selfish	• Taking the best things for him/herself • Not being able to take turns • Doing something even if it makes someone else feel badly	Egocentricity

Positive Response Process

Give Feedback

Make a comment that adds substantive value to one action a child could make in order to improve. For example, if a child grumbles that he is a bad soccer player, don't dismiss his comment, but encourage him to examine one aspect of the task that he can direct his energy toward improving. Perhaps he plays very little soccer and an increased commitment might help: "If we want to improve at something, we need to commit to practicing and working hard at it."

Set Goals

Support students in understanding the skill they lack and how that lack might lie behind their struggles. For example, if a child is always complaining and generally negative, consider supporting her in developing a more optimistic view of the world, first by helping her understand that she notices the bad things more than she notices the good. Set a goal for the student to write down one positive observation a day.

Regulate

If a student gets upset and struggles to control him/herself (e.g., yells, can't sit down, becomes silly, won't stop talking), supporting the child through self-calming should take priority over problem-solving or examining his/her challenges. Help the child to calm down first; do not discuss the issue or tell the child what he/she should be doing. Some students need to be removed from the classroom, not in punishment or reprimand, but because they need a break from the environment to be able to gain control over their bodily reactions. For example, if a child begins to talk so much that he is disrupting a whole group, try telling the student that you need him in the hall for a minute. Once in the hall, get down to the student's level. Tell him that you brought him there to calm his body down, and that, for now, the best way to calm down is to take a break from the situation.

Engage

When a student continues to behave in a problematic way, do not act surprised or disappointed that the student is repeating the dysfunctional behavior. Be prepared to approach the student with the same calm manner you would display for any other student challenge.

Support

Calmly approach students whose behaviors are disruptive and assist them in the self-examination process. See if they can determine one thing that they would like to try to do differently for the rest of the lesson. Allow them to engage in this reflection and come up with the answer on their own. You can refer to previous self-reflection sheets or prompt them by asking them if there is one thing they wish they could do differently.

Of Strengths and Challenges of Others

Objective: To develop a realistic view of the strengths and challenges of others to understand the impact that others have on our relationships.

> Noah is in Grade 4. He struggles with negativity.
>
> Noah has a hard time most days. He is irritable and complains a lot. Noah sees problems and hurdles that most people would let go of or work out in their heads. Lately, Noah has been particularly bothered by and upset with another student. This student suffers from inflexibility issues of her own. She gets stuck on a topic or an idea and tends to go on and on about it; this behavior is noticed by most children in the class, but accepted as something that she is working on. But Noah releases a huge sigh and screams how annoying the other student is because she will not stop talking about a video game.
>
> *Ignore*
> You let Noah vent about the other student. Maybe it will help her with her fixations to have another student tell her how much it bothers him.
>
> *React*
> You tell Noah that he is being rude, that it is not the other student's fault that she gets stuck on a topic. You talk with Noah in private to tell him that she has autism.
>
> *Respond*
> Be ready to support both students through the long process of understanding and accepting the challenges of others while working on their own struggles.

Children are forced to work together and get along with their peers all day long. As teachers, we want to celebrate the diversity of human behavior, just as we celebrate the diversity of race and religion. We want to support students in understanding that each person brings strengths and challenges to every learning and play situation, in the classroom and the playground, and beyond. We all have something to offer, but we are also all working on getting better at things.

We need to support students in recognizing and knowing the strengths and challenges of others. Take the time to allow students to understand each of their classmates, their ways of interacting, speaking, and cooperating. Children often need help understanding the thinking, feeling, and behavior of others and that these ways of being are not the same for everyone. The ways in which students are different will influence the way they act in the classroom.

As we increase students' awareness of the personal strengths and challenges of other students in the class, they might begin to realize that it is the weakness of another that is their trigger, the thing that causes them stress and gets them upset. Chapter 4: Acceptance (page 67) focuses on how we learn to accept and forgive the actions of others and use our understanding of their struggles to improve how we think about challenging situations. But this often needs to start with the recognition of these issues.

Awareness-Building Activity

Daily community circles are a great way to build awareness of the strengths and struggles of others. Through consistent discussions, students learn to listen to the experiences, struggles, and strengths of their classmates in open and nonjudgmental ways.

Community circles can be used with children from Junior Kindergarten to Grade 8. They are simple, daily social-emotional sharing circles with the goal of increasing awareness of ourselves and listening to others. A topic is introduced that requires students to reflect and comment. While each student is talking, the teacher's primary focus and goal is encouraging attentive listening from classmates. Students are not to comment on what others say, only to nod or to say, "Thank you for sharing." Students can ask to pass if they do not want to comment.

Use simple starter questions or themes to guide each discussion:
- *What makes you feel happy?*
- *What is one thing you find hard?*
- *What is something that you don't know how to do, but would like to learn?*

> ### Relationship: Teacher–Teacher
>
> Not all teachers are skilled in all areas of teaching, not only in terms of different subjects, but also in terms of different roles and skill strengths. A strong school is a school that recognizes the strengths of its teachers and acknowledges the areas in which particular teachers are weak, not only for the purpose of improving areas of weakness but, where possible, also to create systems of supporting and working together, pairing and sharing the workload based on the skill strengths of all teachers. For example, a teacher who is highly organized and efficient at data collection and student tracking could assume these responsibilities in the classroom of a coworker who struggles with systems organization; perhaps that colleague enjoys and is proficient with curriculum development and interactive whiteboard lessons, and could undertake those roles in both classrooms. We do not need to work in isolation within our classrooms.

The Positive Response Process

Give Feedback

Allow students to list what upsets them, even if that list includes the actions of other students. Set clear guidelines with the class; i.e., students can list the behaviors of students that upset them without writing names.

SAMPLE LIST

Things that Upset Me
• When someone bites her nails. • When someone taps his desk. • When someone leans into me. • When I do all the work for a group project. • When we have indoor recess. • When someone repeats the same story over and over again. • When gym class is cancelled. • When someone plays the wrong note in music class. • When someone does not know the rules of our game. • When the computer is slow or it does not work.

Set Goals

Students need to work on being aware that everyone in the class has different strengths and challenges and that they must often work together. They must realize that, while working in the groups, they might have variances in their abilities to accomplish certain tasks; sometimes students will work with someone who can do something more easily than they can, and other times they will work with someone who cannot do things as well as they can.

Regulate

When a student becomes upset by the behaviors of others, try not to rush in and problem-solve. Encourage a self-calming strategy; for example, have the students take a step away from each other.

Engage

Be available to a student who is struggling with the challenges of another student. It is not fair to students to dismiss their problems by telling them that it is rude to complain about the struggles of another student or that they need to let it go. Allow students who struggle with the challenging behavior of other students an outlet to express themselves and to feel heard. Sit and listen or provide the student with a writing journal.

Support

Support students in being aware of the strengths and challenges of others without making comments and hurting the feelings of other students in their class. Students need consistent examples of what they can think inside their heads but should not say out loud. Use a self-reflection chart for students who struggle with knowing what they can say out loud and what they should keep inside their heads (see Say It/Don't Say It template on page 44). Students who need some guidance with interaction can complete charts and then use them as reference during group work.

Of Triggers

Objective: To identify the causes of stress in order to understand its impact on ourselves.

> Felix is a Grade 1 student. He struggles with anxiety.
>
> Felix is a mystery to his teachers. He is often calm and very talkative. When he is reading or engaged in a structured and focused activity, he is a knowledgeable little boy who follows the routines of the classroom. But at other times he runs around the room, making funny sounds and odd facial expressions. Then he retreats and hides under a table, where he rocks back and forth, and hums. This behavior occurs when the room is dynamic and busy, or when a new person comes into the class. After multiple meetings with school administration, Felix's parents informed the school that he struggles with anxiety.
>
> *Ignore*
> Now that you know that Felix has anxiety, you give him space to deal with it in his own way.
>
> *React*
> You encourage Felix to come back to the group and join the class during activities. You remove him from under the table. It does not help him to develop unhealthy behaviors to avoid his stress; it is better to expose him to stress so that he learns to deal with it.
>
> *Respond*
> Help Felix apply language and understanding to his experience. Work with him to understand what it is in the environment that upsets him. After he runs under the table and hides, approach him and discuss his behavior: "I wonder if you know why you ran under the table and why you are rocking back and forth. There might have been some kind of change in the classroom that made you feel like you wanted or needed to be under the table. We can work together to figure out what made you want to run and hide." Help him identify the trigger: "When the Grade 8 students came into our class, that's when you went under the table." List his triggers on a piece of paper or in a special notebook where he can record his thoughts and feelings.
>
> **SAMPLE TRIGGER LIST**
>
> | Felix's List of Hard Situations |
> | --- |
> | • New students coming into the class
• Lots of movement on the carpet
• Noise out in the hall
• Group work outside in the hallway |

When stress is easy to identify and understand—i.e., age-appropriate and/or caused by a typical trigger—parents and teachers are often able to support a child through the stress and to make allowances for misbehavior that arises from it. But not all triggers of stress are obvious. Today's triggers are not bears in the woods or survival threats, but are more usually social challenges, school difficulties, or sensory stimuli. The more subtle and less obvious the trigger, the harder it is for both student and teacher to identify it as the cause of the unhealthy behavior. We can support students to become more aware of the environments in which they feel uneasy or upset.

Many of the stress triggers at school revolve around the behavior of other students. Sometimes they are intentional actions, like bullying. But more often they are not intentional actions of others, but a student's own reaction to stress, or clashes in personalities and interests. The most challenging triggers for many students to learn to handle are, in fact, when negative actions or behavior by someone whom they value and trust, such as a close friend or their teacher, violate what they expect from that individual.

Student–Class Relationships

Some children walk onto the playground and appear to lose behavioral control. They run around and bang into other children, or make repetitive noises. If the unpredictability, openness, and noise of the playground elicit feelings of panic and worry in a student, he/she might engage in odd or unhealthy behaviors as a reaction. This cycle is difficult to diagnose. The student will not approach a teacher and say, "I feel nervous because I am unsure where my friends are and I don't know what to do right now." It is our job to observe student behavior and to help them put languge to their actions.

Issues that are appropriate for young children to struggle with continue to be a challenge for some students as they age. They continue to react to triggers after most of their peers have outgrown them; they react strongly to triggers that other children would be upset by but would manage internally. For example, most toddlers struggle with transition and worry when their parents leave them. Kindergarten teachers are accustomed to this, because it is age-appropriate and common. But a Grade 4 student who becomes agitated or irritated during drop-off might not receive the same compassion and support from his/her parents and teacher. Procedures to support this child might not be implemented, and negative feedback could be directed to him/her, further increasing the child's stress at this trigger.

Awareness-Building Activity

Allow all your students to track what they think makes them upset. They can make lists on their own. However, students who have no ability to reflect on their triggers might list triggers that they have heard make others upset; for example a student might say, "I am afraid of heights, dogs, and volcanoes." It is possible that the student is afraid of these things, but also that the student recognizes them as things that other people are afraid of. It is worth examining, without putting ideas into the students' heads, what aspects of the classroom might act as triggers. Provide students with sentences reflecting the triggers that some students in your class are experiencing, and ask them if these scenarios would or would not bother them. Substitute other words for the word *trigger*. Examine what might make them upset, troubled, bothered, or hassled. In time, they can begin to investigate what those words mean.

Distribute copies of the Trigger List (page 43) and the Problem Continuum (page 44) and have students follow these steps:

1. Read the sentences on this list and think about what makes the child in each sentence upset.
2. Underline the words that describe why the child is upset.
3. Pick ten sentences that describe things that might make you upset, or write ten new sentences describing things that would make you upset.
4. Cut out the sentences.
5. Use the Problem Continuum and glue the sentences where you feel they belong, from a Huge Problem to Not a Problem.

The Positive Response Process

Give Feedback

If you figure out a student's trigger, try to give descriptive information that might assist the child in identifying the trigger independently, instead of just telling the student. Use "I wonder…" statements and try to get the student to link events: for example, "I wonder if something set you off this morning You were sitting at the carpet, singing with the group, and then you jumped up and ran out. I wonder if there was something that caused you to jump up and run out."

Set Goals

Assist students in taking more notice of aspects of the classroom, of the time of day, of situations that make them upset. Encourage them to create their own Problem Scales in which they rate challenges that upset them.

In the second sample, the student wrote the name of another student in the class. While working with him, I crossed out the other student's name and indicated that we could just write *classmate* so as not to hurt anyone's feelings.

SAMPLE PROBLEM SCALES

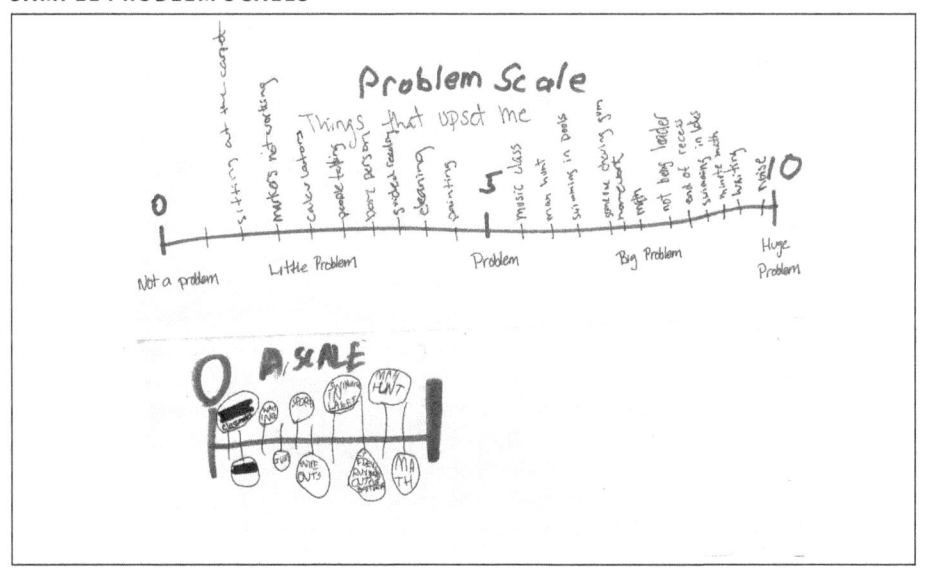

Regulate

Breathing helps calm the body by slowing the heart rate and lowering blood pressure.

Calm students by getting down to their level and looking at them. Nod your head to get their attention, without talking or lecturing. Take exaggerated slow, deep breaths as you speak. Model breathing before you teach it, so that children are interested in and have some understanding of this calming strategy before you use it.

Of Triggers

Engage

Smile and nod at the student who is in distress. Signal that you know that what he/she is going through is hard, but that you will help. Convey understanding and compassion so that the student in crisis believes that he/she is understood.

Support

Proximal support can help empower students. If students are upset and begin to engage in unhealthy behaviors, sometimes simply moving slowly into their space, without negative judgment but with clear intent to help, can calm them.

Teacher–Self Relationship

Are you aware of your triggers? Do you know what category they fall into? Read over the following chart and rate the triggers.

Category	Type	Rate the Stress 1 = no stress 5 = enormous stress
Personal	• Financial • Health • Family • Other: _____	1 2 3 4 5 1 2 3 4 5 1 2 3 4 5 1 2 3 4 5
Teaching Pressures (Teacher–Self)	• Ability to meet teaching expectations • Demands of curriculum content • Documentation, tracking, and reporting • Expectations • Other: _____	1 2 3 4 5 1 2 3 4 5 1 2 3 4 5 1 2 3 4 5 1 2 3 4 5
Interpersonal Staff Dynamics (Teacher–Teacher)	• Co-teaching challenges • Conflict with specific staff members • Distribution and equity of work in the school • Other: _____	1 2 3 4 5 1 2 3 4 5 1 2 3 4 5 1 2 3 4 5
Student Needs (Teacher–Student)	• Challenging students • Needy students • Business and noise of the classroom • Other: _____	1 2 3 4 5 1 2 3 4 5 1 2 3 4 5 1 2 3 4 5

Trigger List

Underline the words that describe why the person in the sentence is upset.

Sample: *The girl was upset because <u>her friend was mad at her</u>.*

- The boy was upset because his friend was better at soccer.
- Don was upset because his brother messed up his room.
- Lisa was upset because she had a hard test.
- Hannah is upset because her friend has better clothes than she does.
- Jenny is upset because another kid on her team is a much better player than she is.
- Daniel was upset because he was made fun of by kids in his class.
- Pam is upset because another student in her class is always telling her what to do.
- Anil is upset because he noticed that a friend of his has stopped speaking to him.
- Jaydon is upset because someone is gossiping about him behind his back.
- Kendra is upset because she got into a fight.
- Summer is upset because someone threatened to hurt her.
- Frank is upset because he gets a lot of homework.
- Anna is upset because her homework is too hard.
- Layla is upset because she has a homework project.
- Tyler is upset because his classroom is very loud.
- Emily is upset because there is a strange humming sound in the classroom.
- Joshua is upset because a kid in his class always shouts.
- Sammy is upset because his music class is learning new instruments and the noise is loud and terrible.
- Angie is upset because someone is tapping his/her foot in the classroom.
- Rob is upset because his partner is sitting too close to him.
- Devin is upset because people expect a lot from him.
- Veronica is upset because she came in second in a race.
- Jazmyn is upset because she did not win her game today.
- Joel is upset because he has to go to math class.
- Leah is upset because she has to go to language class.
- Julie is upset because her class is about to start guided reading.
- Diana is upset because it is time for science class.
- Raymond is upset because it is time for group work.
- Tara is upset because her teacher uses a harsh tone of voice.
- Christina is upset because her teacher talks too fast.
- Thomas is upset because his teacher demands a lot from him.
- Bryan is upset because his mom makes him attend clubs after school.
- Zachary is upset because everyone expects him to be a leader and to excel in everything.
- Kaitlyn is upset because she has too many things she is supposed to do.
- Jeremey is upset because he does not have enough time to himself.

Say It/Don't Say It

I noticed something about my friend.
Should I say something about it?

DON'T SAY IT…	SAY IT…
…if it will make your friend feel sad.	…if it will make your friend feel happy.
Is it ☐ Negative? ☐ Not helpful? ☐ Criticism? ☐ Correction?	Is it ☐ Positive? ☐ Helpful? ☐ Encouraging? ☐ Supportive?
Is my tone of voice ☐ Harsh? ☐ Rough?	Is my tone of voice ☐ Soft? ☐ Gentle?
Is it a time of ☐ High stress?	Is it a time of ☐ Low stress?
If you have more check marks in this column: *I should keep this in my head.*	If you have more check marks in this column: *I could say something to help my friend.*

Problem Continuum

1   2   3   4   5   6   7   8   9   10

Not a problem   Little Problem   Problem   Big Problem   Huge Problem

Of Impact of Stress on the Body

Objective: To examine the ways that stress affects our bodies in order to understand external influences on ourselves.

> Addison is in Grade 4.
>
> Addison often has disagreements and problems with other children. Once she is upset, she yells and screams. Then she seeks out a teacher. When she comes to you, she is agitated and shaky. She screams and yells about what another student did to her.
>
> *Ignore*
> You listen to Addison's version of the story and to the other student's, then you tell them to play on their own.
>
> *React*
> You sternly tell Addison to calm down.
>
> *Respond*
> When Addison tries to speak to you, you gently raise your hands in the air and indicate that she is not ready to speak yet. You draw her attention to the negative power in her body and indicate that she needs to calm down her body before you can think and problem-solve.

External stress triggers launch the body into a Fight, Flight, or Freeze reaction in defence against danger. This has an automatic physical impact on the body. Symptoms might include increased heart rate, shallow breathing, dizziness, sweaty palms, nausea, or headaches. Children are often not aware that it is stress that is causing their physical symptoms. Once they develop negative physical symptoms, they experience stress from two sources: the initial source and the physical symptoms.

If a child understands that stress is causing the physical symptoms, worrying about underlying medical problems will not cause additional stress, and the child is often more motivated to engage in calming strategies to mitigate the physical symptoms of the stress.

Awareness-Building Activities

Stress Curve

Ask students to self-reflect on the sensations in their bodies before and during challenging moments, considering what they look like and the areas of their bodies that react when they become upset. Work with students to plot their low, medium, and high stress on a Stress Curve; see template on page 48.

SAMPLE STRESS CURVE

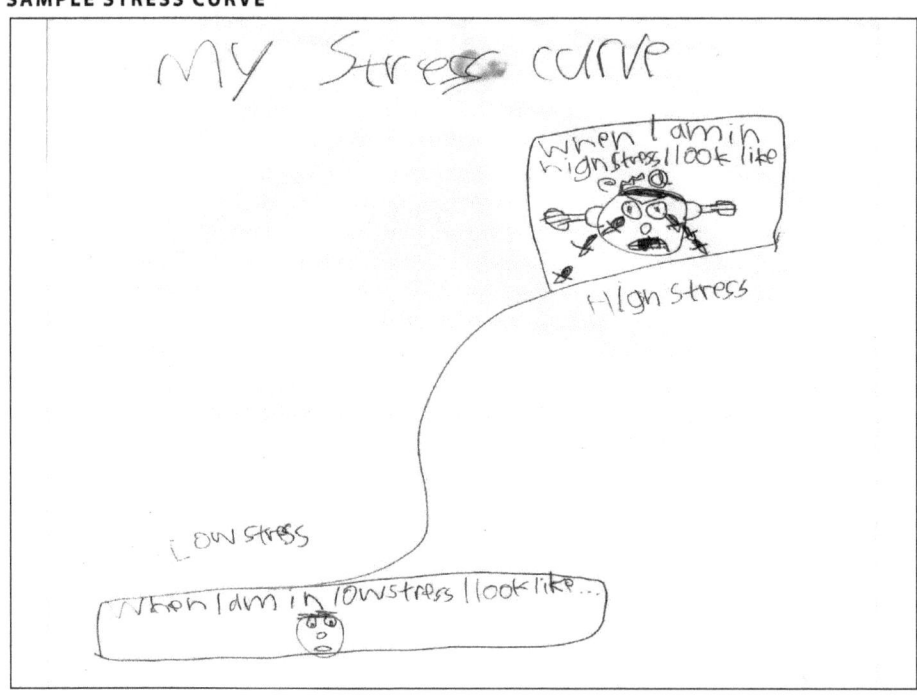

Drawing My Body Under Stress

Some students struggle to know what their body looks like and what physical sensations they experience in states of low, medium, and high stress. Explore this with them by asking them to self-reflect on the sensations in their bodies before, during, and after disagreements or challenging moments, and to draw the sensations on a body outline. Examine what they look like and the areas of their bodies that react when they become upset.

SAMPLE BODY UNDER STRESS

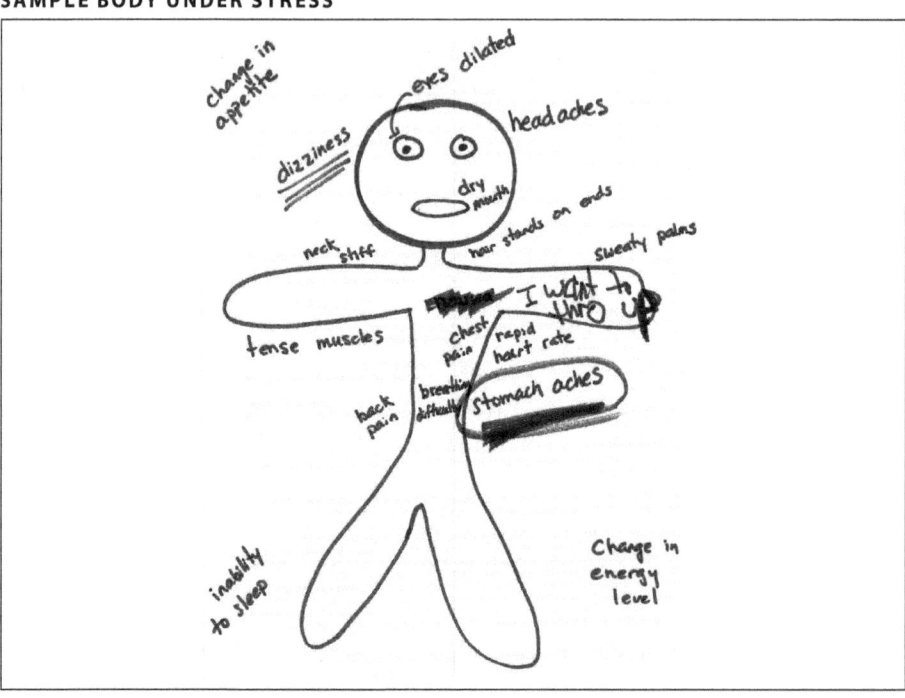

Listing Activity

Work with students to list the physical symptoms they feel when under stress.

SAMPLE LIST OF PHYSICAL SYMPTOMS OF STRESS

- heart racing
- body moves everywhere
- palms sweating
- nausea
- dizziness
- headache
- twitches
- tics
- indigestion
- change in appetite
- chest pains
- dry mouth
- tense muscles
- stiff neck
- breathing problems
- weight loss or gain

The Positive Response Process

Give Feedback

Before starting an activity, ask students to notice the physical sensations their bodies experience during the activity. For example, before language arts, ask students to think about how their head, mouth, shoulders, and stomach feel; if their bodies are sluggish or moving all over the place. Encourage students to track what their bodies look like when they are ready to learn and engaged, as well as when they are not able to listen and are disengaged from the class.

Feedback Activity

Discuss with students the distinction between energy levels and stress levels. Their energy level could be positive or negative, and does not necessarily correspond with whether they are experiencing stress. This activity is an exploration of how their bodies feel and what level of energy they have. Provide students with the My Energy Level chart (page 49) to record the energy level their bodies are at and to draw what their bodies looked like during the school day.

Note that this student indicates a high energy level for recess, but her drawing reveals that this energy manifests as negative behavior; she runs and bumps into other children.

SAMPLE ENERGY LEVEL CHART

Of Impact of Stress on the Body 47

My Stress Curve

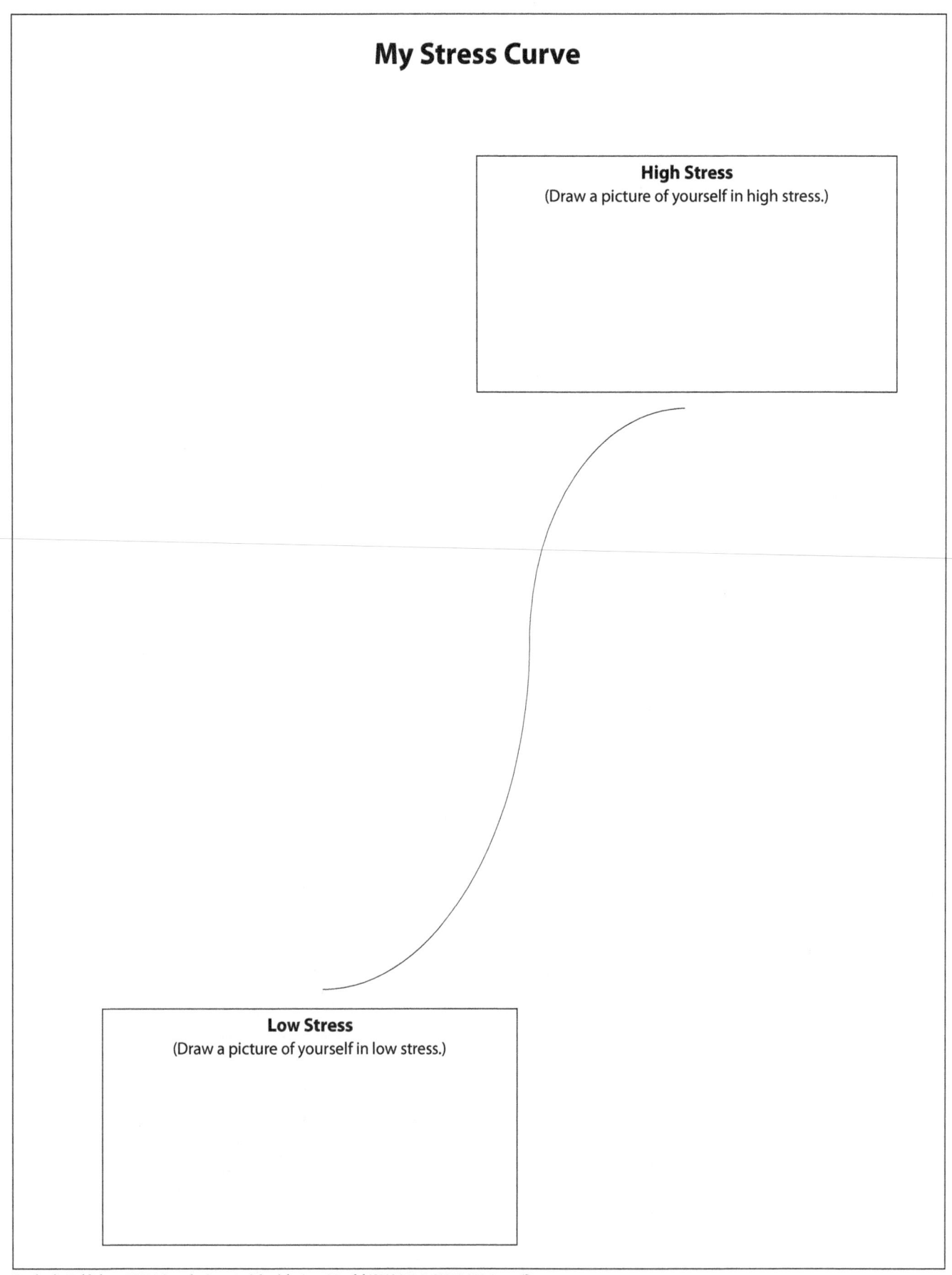

High Stress
(Draw a picture of yourself in high stress.)

Low Stress
(Draw a picture of yourself in low stress.)

My Energy Level

I can track my body's energy level.

Name: _____

Subject	Circle Your Body's Energy Level	Draw How Your Body Looks
Guided Reading	HIGH Medium Low	
Recess	HIGH Medium Low	
Gym	HIGH Medium Low	
Lunch	HIGH Medium Low	
Math	HIGH Medium Low	
Recess	HIGH Medium Low	
Science	HIGH Medium Low	
Home time	HIGH Medium Low	

Body Stress Curve

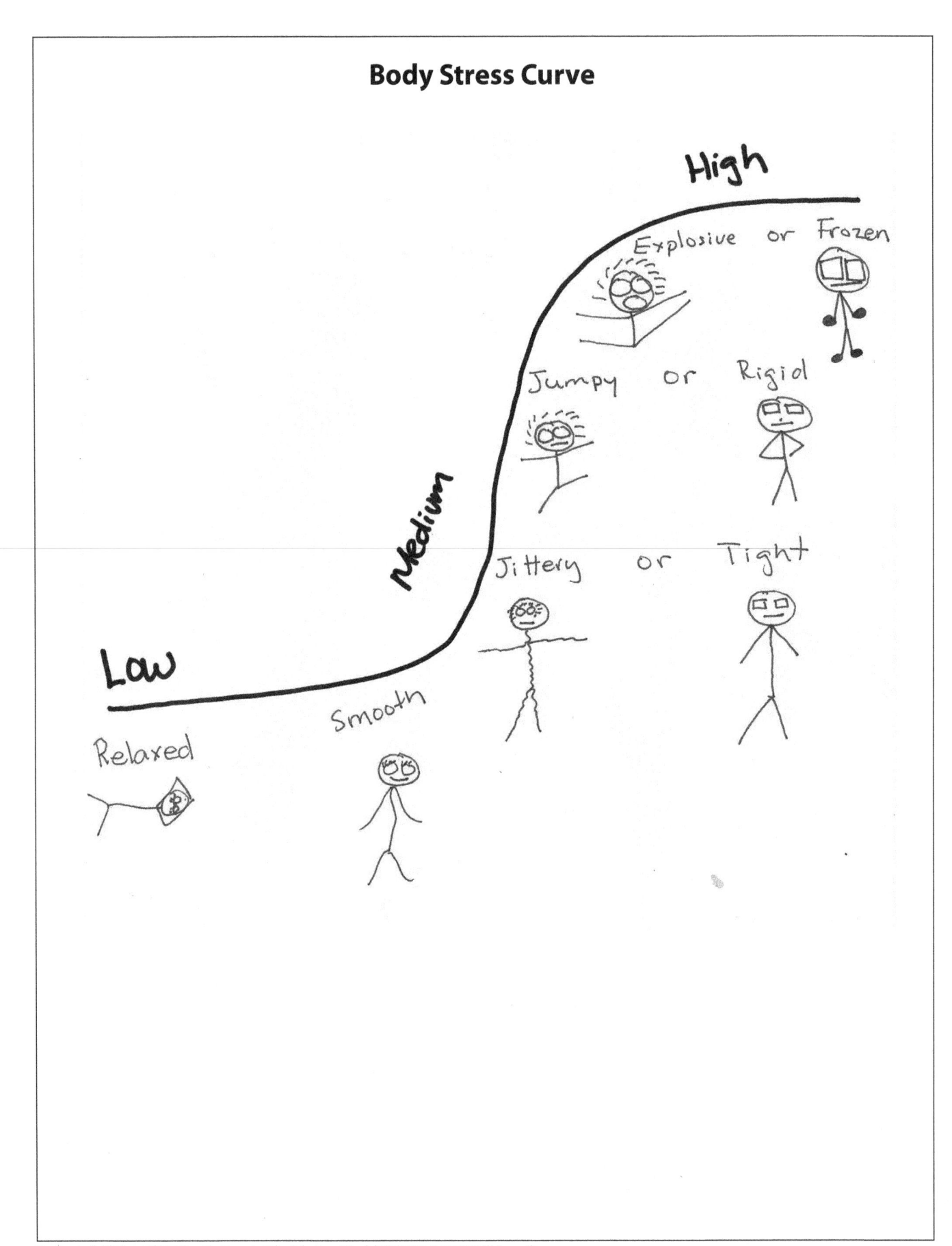

High

Explosive or Frozen

Jumpy or Rigid

Medium

Jittery or Tight

Low

Smooth

Relaxed

Set Goals

Students need to learn the difference between sensations in their bodies when they are relaxed and how they feel when they are tense or upset. With practice, they will be able to track the way their bodies react when they are upset.

Regulate

Begin to introduce self-calming strategies with students any time they come to you upset. Signal for them to Stop: i.e., to ground themselves, plant their feet, and stop talking. When they are in a state of upset, do not listen to their arguments or try to problem-solve; tell them, "You need to slow down and self-calm first." The point of grounding is to support students to stop moving, talking, and trying to explain or defend themselves; these behaviors cause agitation and increase stress.

Engage

When you see students becoming upset, smile at them and model a self-calming technique. Stop moving, plant your feet, put your hands at your side, close your eyes, and breathe in slowly. This method of engagement has two advantages: it will help calm you down before you react; it does not put any demands on students, but simply shows them a way to manage stress.

Support

Once students are calm, ask each of them how they feel, now that they have calmed their bodies and taken the time to relax. Show each student a Body Stress Curve (page 50) and ask them to point to where he/she thinks his/her body is.

Of Impact of Stress on Behavior

Objective: To become more aware of how we react when we experience stress.

> London is in Grade 4. She has an intolerance of uncertainty, and struggles with social anxiety.
>
> Even in art class, London seems to need you to explain assignments over and over again. She asks repeated questions about the exact way you envision the work and want her to complete it, about the way it should be done. She is unable to start her work until you have explained it a few times and shown her examples, including what the other children have begun.
>
> *Ignore*
> You understand that London struggles with anxiety, so you give her the detail and explanations she needs. You walk her through step-by-step and show her as many examples as you can to facilitate her process.
>
> *React*
> The pressure to answer multiple questions you have not planned for stresses you out. You point London back to her seat and tell her that she is asking too many questions about the assignment.

> *Respond*
> Help London link her behavior to her anxiety. Make a chart with her that lists her triggers and the questions that pop into her head once she becomes upset. Assist her in keeping track of these questions. In the future, you could assist her in identifying her thinking through her questions.

The Fight, Flight, or Freeze reaction releases stress hormones into the brain. This stress is supposed to be temporary and acute, in reaction to extreme danger; but for those who experience more chronic stress, the effects of stress accumulate in the body. Their brains begin to change in response to the stress hormones. The pathways that allow dopamine (positive hormones) to the brain begin to decrease as the pathways that facilitate stress hormones are used more and more. The brain–body connection of children who experience a lot of stress gets wired to a negative response.

The brain also responds to Fight, Flight, or Freeze by shutting down its pathways to the neocortex, the thinking part of the brain. The stressed child enters a physical reactive state and does not have the ability to problem-solve, learn, or listen. The child is not in a thinking or reflective state in which he/she can access previously learned information or apply what he/she knows to work through the challenges of a situation. This is why we witness unhealthy and inappropriate behaviors in a stressed child. These behaviors are reactive behaviors; they are not thought out or planned. When a child misbehaves, it is essential for us to understand that no thinking was involved in the behavior, that it was reactive.

Children seek to control their environments by avoidance, using explosive behavior: e.g., yelling, being defiant, being aggressive. This kind of disruption gets noticed and steps are often taken to prevent or minimize the behavior. However, when stress is manifested in less extreme or disruptive ways—e.g., jumping in, dictating to those around them, giving instructions or asking repeated questions—the behavior is often not examined. It is seen as part of the child's way of acting, and is possibly just accepted as annoying or irritating behavior. The anxiety underlying the behavior is not addressed, so the behavior is not effective in reducing the child's anxiety. Moreover, it can cause stress and irritation in other people. It begins a cycle: a child feels anxious, engages in behavior designed to reduce anxiety (but does not); the behavior causes stress in other people and might result in unpleasant interactions, further increasing the child's stress.

Often one student's trigger is the action of another student during their own stress; for example, a student yelling at recess or screaming at another student when upset can trigger that second student's stress.

> ### Relationship: Teacher–Class
>
> Stress cycles emerge in classrooms every day. One person experiences stress from his/her trigger, and then reacts to the stress, displaying negative behavior toward another student. This behavioral response acts as a trigger for the second student, whose stress reaction is directed toward yet another student. As teachers, we also play a part in this vicious cycle. We come into our classroom in states of heightened stress, worried about the amount of work we need to cover or frustrated by the behaviors of certain students. If we react to that stress by snapping at students, by yelling at or reprimanding them, we increase the level of stress in our whole classroom.

Awareness-Building Activities

Questioning

One behavior a lot of people demonstrate when they are stressed is asking a lot of questions. But asking questions is, in fact, the most functional behavior students can engage in, because it can help us understand their thinking. Students who ask a lot of questions are detailing their thinking out loud. Allow students to ask their questions and assist them in using their questions in order to track their thinking.

On the interactive whiteboard, brainstorm with students to list possible questions they might ask out loud when they feel stressed or upset.

SAMPLE QUESTION CHART

Trigger	Questions I Might Ask Out Loud
Given an assignment in class	*How to do it?* *How long?* *What format?* *When is it due?* *Will it be marked?* *Will we present it?*
Recess time	*What do my friends want to play?* *Who is going out for recess?* *Where will we play?* *Do they want to play with me?* *Did my friends think yesterday's game was fun?* *Do they really like me?*
My friend looks mad	*What did I do?* *Did I say something to hurt her feelings?* *Does she think I said something to hurt her feelings?* *Did someone else do or say something mean?* *Can I help her?* *Should I tell her that I did not do anything?* *Should I tell her that someone else was laughing at her behind her back yesterday?*
Playing basketball	*What will the teams be?* *Will the teacher pick teams or will the students pick?* *Will I get picked last?* *What if I trip?* *What if I miss a shot?* *Why do we have to play this?*

Identifying Triggers

Have students list their triggers, as well as the behaviors they engage in when they experience the triggers.

SAMPLE TRIGGERS→BEHAVIOR LIST

Triggers

- someone sitting close to me
- recess time
- a new person coming into the room
- loud noise
- someone correcting me
- someone looking at me funny
- tests
- work
- rude voices
- large spaces
- repetitive noises
- pressure
- interruption
- working with someone who is not good at school
- working with someone who is bossy
- animals
- not having enough time for myself

What I Do

- yell
- bump into other kids
- stop talking
- hit other kids
- stop working
- put my head on my desk
- sleep a lot
- try to control everything
- ask a lot of questions
- run away
- disrupt the class
- stop coming to school
- try to organize everything
- make rules for everyone
- try to make things perfect
- cling to someone
- demand that my friends be and act a certain way

Putting It All Together

Using the Stress Makes Me… chart on page 55, encourage students to track their triggers and behaviors, and then to list the questions that they would ask.

SAMPLE STRESS MAKES ME… CHART

Trigger	Behavior	Question
Loud noise	Yelled at the student making noise	*Why won't she stop?*
Saw my two friends playing together without me	Went up to them and told them they were annoying	*Why didn't they include me?*
Time to go to music class	Left my class and walked around the school	*What if I can't do well in music?*
Grade 8 students came to our class to visit	Went to the back of the class, sat down on the floor, and refused to do any work	*Why do they have to be here in my classroom?*

The Positive Response Process

Give Feedback

Examine with students their Stress Makes Me… charts. Assist them in understanding why they behave in a particular way.

Stress Makes Me...

Trigger	Behavior	Question

Have each student create a special Thinking and Feeling book in which to keep track of their growing awareness of themselves and others.

Set Goals

Students must learn to catch themselves engaging in behaviors because of a trigger. Encourage students to record the trigger and their resulting behavior in a Thinking and Feeling notebook.

Regulate

The process of thinking about and recording their behaviors helps students in their personal recognition of their triggers, and also provides them with a calming activity that diverts their attention from their triggers. The act of opening up a book and writing or drawing gives them a voice and calms them down.

Engage

Remind yourself that the misbehavior of the student is not intentional or controlled. This might help you approach the student with more positive and less negative energy.

Support

Clarify with students that they need to learn strategies to manage and control dysfunctional behaviors, but that the behaviors do not represent who they are as individuals. For example, some children who become upset and use mean words when under stress have low self-esteem and will call themselves "mean" or "bad." It is important for them to understand that their reaction to stress gets them into trouble, but that they themselves are not mean, irritating, or bad.

Of Impact of Stress on Thinking

Objective: To examine the impact of stress on our personal thinking about self and others.

> Derek is in Grade 6. He struggles with social anxiety.
>
> Derek has a few good friends, but he is always worried about what they think of him. Derek is aware that sometimes he is awkward around his friends and that he can say the wrong thing. Since he has learned that he has social anxiety, he understands it as the cause of some of his social struggles and is obsessed with discussing his social struggles and his social anxiety. He tells you that he feels nervous about going out at recess and that he feels unsure of what to do or say. He wonders what others will think of him. He keeps telling you that he just wants other people to like him and to think kindly of him.
>
> *Ignore*
> You encourage Derek to talk with you about his problems and welcome him walking with you at recess to share his worries and his concerns. By doing this, you are not ignoring Derek; you are ignoring the issue that is causing is anxiety and not supporting him through it.
>
> *React*
> You know that Derek plays well with other kids and that they are often nice to him. You tell him to go in and join the group.

> *Respond*
> Guide Derek to recognize that he is not using his awareness of his own anxiety to help him develop tools to beat it, but rather is becoming more anxious about it. Sit with Derek after a challenging experience. Help him understand that he might struggle with negative thinking, but that together you can track the negative thinking and work through it.

Core beliefs set the stage for how we feel and behave in each situation. Some people are predisposed to optimistic and positive thinking. For these people, the glass truly is half-full. Their brains are preconfigured to see good in the world, in others, and in each situation. When they are in threatening or difficult situations, they tend toward positive thinking because their underlying core beliefs are optimistic. Others are born with a tendency toward pessimistic thinking. Their natural core beliefs are negative or even destructive. These beliefs affect the way they perceive and interpret each event. For these people, the glass is half-empty in each and every situation. They are naturally predisposed to think "I can't"—a frame of mind that can significantly reduce the functioning of a child at home and at school.

Negative thinking is often reactive or automatic; in cognitive behavior therapy they are called Hot Thoughts. Hot Thoughts are what go through our minds when we are having strong feelings and reactions; they occur quickly, without clear processing and analysis. Most people who have negative Hot Thoughts tend to interpret a situation negatively in the following ways:

- Mind-reading: Assuming and inferring reasons behind someone else's actions and thinking
- Catastrophizing: Believing that the worst possible outcome will occur
- All or Nothing: Thinking in absolute terms; e.g., the outcome will be one thing, or the situation would never happen
- Overgeneralization: Taking something that happened once and assuming the same outcome will continue to happen
- Mental Filtering: Focusing on only the negatives of a situation
- Disqualifying the Positives: Coming up with reasons why a positive explanation or option is not possible
- Jumping to Conclusions: Finding problems where there aren't any

Often children believe that they feel something when what they have is, in fact, a thought; for example, a student might say, "I felt like I did not want to go to music class." That is not a feeling, but is a thought that could lead to a feeling or mood. It is important for students to be able to distinguish between thoughts and feelings. It is necessary to assist students in recognizing their patterns of thinking, because these patterns are the basis for what they feel and how they behave, day in and day out. Their behaviors affect each relationship they form.

Awareness-Building Activity

A thought record notes the thoughts that pop into an individual's head. It is a way to record and examine the internal thinking of a student.

Speak in class about different ways of thinking about events to help students identify how they tend to think. Using thought records, track with students the thoughts that pop into their heads in various situations. Let students trace the incrementally negative thinking that can build from the first negative thought.

With students, make thought records that depict increased negative thinking. Explain that once an individual engages in negative thinking, it spirals and becomes more and more negative. If this is how students think, how will this thinking affect their behavior?

SAMPLE OF A NEGATIVE THOUGHT RECORD

Situation	First Thought	Next Thought	Next Thought
We have to present our book reports tomorrow.	*I am not very good at speaking in front of others.*	*I bet I will forget my lines.*	*Everyone will laugh at me.*

Teacher–Self Relationship

As teachers, we can also fall victim to negative core beliefs and begin an incremental cycle of negative thinking. This thinking will influence the way we feel and behave at work, with our students and our colleagues, slowly eroding the positive classroom climate we want to sustain.

SAMPLE OF NEGATIVE THOUGHT RECORD

Situation	First Thought	Next Thought	Next Thought
Principal calls a staff meeting to discuss problems in yard duty.	*She is going to talk about the time I was late for yard duty.*	*Everybody always singles me out.*	*Nobody likes me.*

As teachers, it is important to examine our personal patterns of negative thinking. Examples of negative thoughts include

- *I am never going to get through this lesson.*
- *I have so much work to do after school today.*
- *I did not plan this lesson well enough.*
- *I don't know what I am doing.*
- *Other teachers are better than I am.*
- *The kids don't care.*
- *Why don't my colleagues do more work?*
- *What is wrong with this kid?*
- *Don't this child's parents spend any time with him?*
- *Why do I even bother?*
- *The school system is overburdened and can't support these kids.*

If our thinking is dominated by positive and balanced thoughts, things will appear more hopeful and challenges more manageable. Example of positive thinking include

- *This is a hard job, but I can do it.*
- *My role is not to change the world, but to support the children in this room as well as I can.*
- *I am good at my job.*
- *I helped at least one child today.*
- *When I smiled at that student, it meant a lot to him/her.*

Remember that the way we approach a situation will construct the mood we take on to address it.

The Positive Response Process

Give Feedback

> Provide students with positive thinking that they can use to encourage themselves and to view a situation differently.

Just prior to beginning an activity that your students tend to complain about, help them identify some of the negative comments and thinking they might have. Use the interactive whiteboard to draw a stick figure and write a title: *What I Might Be Thinking.* Draw thought bubbles from the stick figure and write the internal thoughts that students suggest.

SAMPLE *WHAT I MIGHT BE THINKING*

> For this sample, students were asked to brainstorm what a person might think when a new student walks into class. The teacher wrote down all the thoughts the students offered, without commenting on them or classifying them as positive or negative.

[Illustration: Stick figure with thought bubbles. Title: "What I might be thinking." Situation: A new student comes in the classroom. Thoughts: "Great! Someone new to play with."; "He looks fun. I love his shirt."; "He will probably take my friends."; "I bet he will be better at basketball than I am."]

Set Goals

Students need to gain awareness of their internal thinking patterns. Then they can begin to observe if their patterns of thinking are positive or negative. Make a thought record with students that highlights the difference between positive and negative thinking.

SAMPLE THOUGHT RECORD

Positive Thought: *I can…*	Negative Thought: *I can't…*
I know that I can do it.	*I can't do this.*
It will work out.	*Things are not going to work out.*
Things will be okay.	*This is going to be terrible.*

Regulate

When students make negative statements, such as "I hate this activity, it is so boring," tell them to catch their negative thinking. Have them stand up and write it in a thought bubble somewhere in the room. The simple acts of standing up, walking through the classroom, and writing down their thinking is an excellent first step in students' awareness, and ultimately management, of negative thinking.

Engage

Some students might not move independently to place their thought bubbles, so you could go with them. While walking with them, do not comment about what they are thinking; instead, try to comment on one positive thing that has nothing to do with the event itself: for example, "Looks like the rain went away so we will still get to have outdoor recess."

Support

Begin to introduce more positive thinking to your students, without having expectations that they will comment or answer a question. If students say something negative, approach them slowly. Empathize with them: for example, say, "That must be frustrating," tilting your head to the side; "That is one way of looking at this problem, but I worry that it is the negative way. I am going to look a little more closely to see if I can notice any good things about this situation."

Of Impact of Stress on Feelings

Objective: To begin to understand the underlying mood we experience when we are upset.

Asher is in Grade 5.

Asher is a creative kid who is accomplished in art and writing. He is often engaged and active in class, beginning most days smiling and energetic. But he can quickly disengage. He becomes withdrawn and noncompliant, and this mood often seems to come out of nowhere. When you give the class a writing assignment, Asher begins it immediately and appears eager to work until he is asked to edit or take feedback from you. Then he becomes disengaged and upset.

Ignore
You figure that all children have ups and downs that lead to extreme behaviors; you don't perceive this as a big deal. You allow Asher to leave his writing assignment incomplete.

React
When Asher is down and low, you point out to him how different his behavior is from previous times, and ask him what is up.

Respond
Realize that Asher's extreme moods are possibly caused by negative thinking and that you can play a role in supporting Asher to find more moderate thinking in his daily life.

A mood is a temporary state of mind or feeling. Often, a mood is one word used to describe how we feel. Moods differ from emotions in that moods are less specific and less intense. Moods are typically either positive or negative, "good" or "bad." (Greenberger and Padesky, 1995)

The thoughts we experience in times of stress define the moods we experience. If our thinking is positive, if we believe that we can achieve our goal or that the problem is not so bad, then we are liable to feel capable, confident, enthusiastic, and optimistic. If our automatic thoughts are negative, then we will experience a negative mood.

The way students think affects the way they feel. It is important to understand that the same negative thought might result in different moods for different students: for example, thinking "Nobody likes me and everyone is out to get me" might make one child feel sad, but would make another child feel angry.

Awareness-Building Activities

With Students

> It is helpful to have a variety of vocabulary words for emotion to use when examining the different emotions with children. See the Mood Chart on page 63.

1. Ask students, *How do you feel when something happens that bothers you?*
2. Have them look at the Student Survey on pages 64–65: *The examples might or might not be triggers for you, but take a look at the different emotional reactions stressful events can cause. Look at the different moods, and consider the mood that you might take on if this situation happened to you.*

Teacher–Self Relationship

Our thinking influences our moods. If our thoughts are positive, our emotions will likely be positive and optimistic as well. Examine the Positive/Negative Thoughts charts. Consider which patterns of thinking you tend to experience. Notice how the type of thinking you do affects the mood you experience.

SAMPLE POSITIVE/NEGATIVE THOUGHTS

Positive Thoughts: *I can…*	**Positive Emotion**
Being kind to and supporting this child, here and now, is the most I can do.	Mindfulness
I can handle this. *I can support this child.*	Confidence
This child has a lot of struggles; my job is to support this child in them.	Empathy
The school staff will support me.	Optimism

Negative Thoughts: *I can't…*	**Negative Emotion**
I know I should be doing more for this child. *If I had modified my lesson, this student would be doing better.* *I was supposed to set up a meeting to get this student a diagnosis.*	Guilt
Why isn't anyone helping me with this child? *What is wrong with his/her parents? Do they even care?* *Why do I always get the hardest classes?*	Anger
No one in the school supports me. *What is the resource teacher doing?* *Don't we have a school social worker to handle this?*	Frustration
This child has serious mental health problems. *There is nothing that can be done for this child.*	Sadness

These are only a few examples of negative thinking. What they have in common is that the underlying motivation is the best interest of the student; however, the personal burden and pressure the teacher places on him/herself causes negative emotion and stress.

For Teachers

The type of thinking we experience leads to positive and negative moods. But not everyone experiences the same type of mood, even if their thinking is similar. Use the Thought-to-Mood for Teachers chart on page 66. Read over the negative thinking patterns. Based on the thinking in the example, what type of mood do you think you would take on?

The Positive Response Process

Give Feedback

On chart paper or the interactive whiteboard, allow students to track their thinking and their moods. Throughout the day, have them record times when they catch themselves thinking positively and its impact on their mood, and times when they are thinking negatively and its impact on their mood.

Set Goals

Help children catch their thinking and link it to different moods that they experience. Assist students in being able to indentify that, if they are in a bad mood, it is because they are thinking negatively.

Regulate

Expand self-calming processes for students when they experience negative moods by practicing deep breathing. Teach children deep-breathing activities with visual imagery (see page 97).

Engage

Assist students in noticing the type of bad mood they experience and the reason for that mood. If a student says "I am angry," help the child recognize that it might not actually be anger he/she is feeling, but worry or fear of an event.

Support

Paraphrase thinking through a problem for students when they are in negative states and engage in dysfunctional behavior. For example, if a student under stress yells, "Get out of my way, you jerk!" don't get sidetracked by the negative language, but give the student more functional language that serves a purpose: "I need a minute right now because I feel overwhelmed."

Mood Chart

Note: Each column shows connected moods.

Negative Moods

Hurt	Worried	Irritated	Offended	Dishonored	Resentful
Sad	Scared	Annoyed	Sickened	Shamed	Begrudging
Disappointed	Nervous	Angry	Disgusted	Embarrassed	Jealous
Miserable	Anxious	Enraged	Revolted	Disgraced	Envious
Depressed	Panicky	Livid	Repulsed	Humiliated	
Apathetic	Frightened	Furious	Appalled	Degraded	

Positive Moods

Self-sufficient	Happy	Content	Grateful	Hopeful
Confident	Cheerful	Calm	Appreciative	Optimistic
Proud	Amused	Peaceful	Thankful	Expectant
Capable	Merry	Refreshed		Enthusiastic
Able	Delighted	Relieved		Passionate
Assured	Ecstatic	Comforted		

Pembroke Publishers ©2014 *Stop the Stress in Schools* by Joey Mandel ISBN 978-1-55138-298-2

Student Survey

Someone in your class is tapping his/her foot and making noise; it helps him/her concentrate. You think…
This noise is unbearable. Will it ever stop? You feel
   Sympathetic   Irritated   Angry   Anxious   Excited   Frustrated   Hopeful   Happy
Why do kids always do things to bug me? You feel
   Sympathetic   Irritated   Angry   Anxious   Excited   Frustrated   Hopeful   Happy
If I distract my brain, it will not bother me as much. You feel
   Sympathetic   Irritated   Angry   Anxious   Excited   Frustrated   Hopeful   Happy
I guess the tapping somehow helps him/her. You feel
   Sympathetic   Irritated   Angry   Anxious   Excited   Frustrated   Hopeful   Happy

Your partner keeps interrupting you when you are speaking. You think…
He/she is so rude. You feel
   Sympathetic   Irritated   Angry   Anxious   Excited   Frustrated   Hopeful   Happy
He/she should listen to me. You feel
   Sympathetic   Irritated   Angry   Anxious   Excited   Frustrated   Hopeful   Happy
Sometimes I interrupt people too. You feel
   Sympathetic   Irritated   Angry   Anxious   Excited   Frustrated   Hopeful   Happy
Maybe he/she has something important to say. You feel
   Sympathetic   Irritated   Angry   Anxious   Excited   Frustrated   Hopeful   Happy

When you play outside, your friend makes all the decisions. You think…
He/she is very controlling. You feel
   Sympathetic   Irritated   Angry   Anxious   Excited   Frustrated   Hopeful   Happy
This is the way he/she plays, but he/she is still a good friend. You feel
   Sympathetic   Irritated   Angry   Anxious   Excited   Frustrated   Hopeful   Happy
This is not fair, I have rights too. You feel
   Sympathetic   Irritated   Angry   Anxious   Excited   Frustrated   Hopeful   Happy
Maybe I can explain to him/her that I get ideas too. You feel
   Sympathetic   Irritated   Angry   Anxious   Excited   Frustrated   Hopeful   Happy

When you stand in line for class, someone bumps into you. You think…
I am going to tell the teacher so he/she gets into trouble. You feel
   Sympathetic   Irritated   Angry   Anxious   Excited   Frustrated   Hopeful   Happy
I sometimes do that by accident too. You feel
   Sympathetic   Irritated   Angry   Anxious   Excited   Frustrated   Hopeful   Happy
That's okay; he/she often bangs into people by accident. It is not his/her fault. He/she just moves too fast. You feel
   Sympathetic   Irritated   Angry   Anxious   Excited   Frustrated   Hopeful   Happy
Why is everyone always trying to hurt me? You feel
   Sympathetic   Irritated   Angry   Anxious   Excited   Frustrated   Hopeful   Happy

Your project partner is a bad speller. You think…
Why do I have to work with the worst partner? You feel
   Sympathetic   Irritated   Angry   Anxious   Excited   Frustrated   Hopeful   Happy
That's okay. He/she is an amazing artist, so he/she can draw our cover page. You feel
   Sympathetic   Irritated   Angry   Anxious   Excited   Frustrated   Hopeful   Happy
We are going to get a terrible mark because of him/her. You feel
   Sympathetic   Irritated   Angry   Anxious   Excited   Frustrated   Hopeful   Happy
This is great. I am not very good at this subject, so I can help him/her with his/her spelling and we will do well together. You feel
   Sympathetic   Irritated   Angry   Anxious   Excited   Frustrated   Hopeful   Happy

Student Survey (continued)

You have a test coming up. You think…
I can do it. You feel

| Sympathetic | Irritated | Angry | Anxious | Excited | Frustrated | Hopeful | Happy |

It will be hard, but I can try. You feel

| Sympathetic | Irritated | Angry | Anxious | Excited | Frustrated | Hopeful | Happy |

There is no way I can ever do this. You feel

| Sympathetic | Irritated | Angry | Anxious | Excited | Frustrated | Hopeful | Happy |

Everyone else finds things easy. You feel

| Sympathetic | Irritated | Angry | Anxious | Excited | Frustrated | Hopeful | Happy |

Thought-to-Mood for Teachers

A child does not know the answer to a question. I think…
What is wrong with this kid?
Mood: Sympathy Sadness Anger Guilt Anxiety _____
Nobody listens to me.
Mood: Sympathy Sadness Anger Guilt Anxiety _____
Every kid has strengths and challenges.
Mood: Sympathy Sadness Anger Guilt Anxiety _____
Why do I even bother?
Mood: Sympathy Sadness Anger Guilt Anxiety _____

A child scrapes his/her knee on the playground and cries uncontrollably. I think…
This child needs to toughen up.
Mood: Sympathy Sadness Anger Guilt Anxiety _____
I hope if my child falls on the playground, someone is there to comfort him/her.
Mood: Sympathy Sadness Anger Guilt Anxiety _____
I can help this child feel better.
Mood: Sympathy Sadness Anger Guilt Anxiety _____
No one helps me when I am hurt.
Mood: Sympathy Sadness Anger Guilt Anxiety _____

A child keeps bumping into other children on the playground. I think…
Why doesn't the administration do anything to support us at recess?
Mood: Sympathy Sadness Anger Guilt Anxiety _____
The school had better find a way to get mental health treatment for this child.
Mood: Sympathy Sadness Anger Guilt Anxiety _____
Why isn't the other teacher on yard duty doing anything?
Mood: Sympathy Sadness Anger Guilt Anxiety _____
I have told this child a million times to be careful.
Mood: Sympathy Sadness Anger Guilt Anxiety _____
It is going to be a long process to help this child, but I can do my best.
Mood: Sympathy Sadness Anger Guilt Anxiety _____

My colleague gave me the wrong information about the staff meeting. I think…
Everybody makes mistakes.
Mood: Sympathy Sadness Anger Guilt Anxiety _____
Now my principal thinks I am incompetent and that don't care about the meeting.
Mood: Sympathy Sadness Anger Guilt Anxiety _____
These types of things always happen to me.
Mood: Sympathy Sadness Anger Guilt Anxiety _____
Everyone else managed to get to the meeting on time, why can't I ever figure things out?
Mood: Sympathy Sadness Anger Guilt Anxiety _____
I will figure out a better system for next time.
Mood: Sympathy Sadness Anger Guilt Anxiety _____

4

Acceptance

Acceptance is essential to the process of stress management because it maintains regulation and prevents further escalation up the stress curve. Increased awareness of stress can lead to increased anxiety if it is not taught in tandem with forgiveness of self and others. By teaching acceptance, we can avoid a cycle of increased negative emotions (guilt, sadness, or anger) when challenges arise. In this chapter, we will examine acceptance of

- self and our own strengths and challenges
- the strengths and challenges of others
- the situation
- the thinking of others
- the need to adapt
- the behavior of others

Of Self

Objective: To teach self-forgiveness and acceptance of the whole self.

> Mark is in Grade 4.
>
> Mark is a fun and exciting student, dynamic and full of life. Most of the time he is extremely kind and caring to classmates; however, at times he makes rude comments and sometimes uses inappropriate language. From the corner of the room, you hear Mark's voice yelling a swear word to another student. You approach him and ask to speak with him. He adamantly denies that he said anything and vows that it was not him.
>
> *Ignore*
> You know that he is not telling the truth, but you accept his answer and indicate that you hope that everyone is being honest.
>
> *React*
> You tell him that you know that he is lying, and do not let him participate in the next fun activity until he admits what he did.
>
> *Respond*
> Bring Mark to your desk and speak with him privately. Support him in understanding that we all make mistakes, that the most important part of making mistakes is being able to forgive ourselves and not engage in more unhealthy behavior, such as lying, to try to protect ourselves.

We want to support our students in self-examination. But if it is done in a critical or judgmental environment, we will create anxiety and further diminish a child's capacity to function. When children are aware of their struggles, and embarrassed or ashamed of them, they will exert time and energy trying to hide and avoid those struggles. Shame, guilt, and embarrassment show that children are tremendously hard on themselves and, in turn, often hard on others. We want our students to be aware and open about challenges, with the confidence of knowing that they are still valued and accepted. We need to empower students to work on their challenges, instead of being consumed by them.

If we examine these situations, students learn to acknowledge their own strengths and what challenges them. This is better done when we separate the examination of self from immediate involvement in strategies to stop the undesirable behavior or "fix" the self. One can be a good person—a good teacher, friend, student, or child—and still make mistakes, make bad choices, and even have challenging behaviors. Self-acceptance involves recognizing mistakes, imperfections, and personal weaknesses and shortcomings.

The negative feelings of blame, guilt, shame, and embarrassment are tied to a lack of self-acceptance. We can soothe feelings of shame by using positive self-talk and encouraging ourselves. Help your students create acceptance to reduce their shame, guilt, and embarrassment. If students can accept and forgive themselves, they will put less energy into their attempts to hide, cover up, and avoid situations in which others see their flaws.

Acceptance-Building Activity

Support students through the process of identifying their initial thinking as positive or negative, and focusing on a positive way of looking at the problem. Use thought records (see page 57) to prompt and support students; it can be extremely helpful for students to create thought records of their own when issues recur.

SAMPLE STUDENT THOUGHT RECORD

Situation	Negative Thought	Positive Self-Talk
While playing together at recess, you and a friend get into an argument.	*He is so mad at me he won't ever speak to me again.*	*We are good friends. All friends fight sometimes, but there are steps that I can take to solve this problem.*

Model using thought records of your own to come to an acceptance of your strengths and weaknesses.

SAMPLE TEACHER THOUGHT RECORD

Situation	Negative Thought	Positive Self-Talk
While writing an assignment on the board, you make a spelling mistake that a student catches and corrects.	*How terrible. If my students tell their parents, the parents will worry about the competency of the person teaching their children.*	*No worries. It is good to show your students that you make mistakes too.*

The Positive Response Process

Give Feedback

Link a student's behavior to their self-criticism; for example, "When you make a mistake or do something that you should not, your next steps will probably be to try to hide your actions or cover up imperfections that others might see. Right now, I think that you are being hardest on yourself. It must be hard to always try to do things perfectly. I think that you spend a lot of effort throughout the day thinking about what other people think of you."

Set Goals

Children need to know that no one is perfect and that everyone makes mistakes. They must see that it is okay to make a mistake. Help students to follow a process that starts with telling themselves that it is okay that they made a mistake, and that the bad things they worry about might not happen.

Regulate

Encourage students to take a deep breath with you and to think of three positive things about themselves. Then have them take another deep breath and tell themselves that, even when they make mistakes, these three positive things are still true and are what people think about them.

Engage

Observe students when they make a mistake or a poor choice and monitor your response to their negative actions or behavior. Control your negative nonverbal reactions of disapproval. It is important to control your nonverbal messaging as much as what you say to your students, as body language is powerful and effective tool in classroom management. Use a gentle and firm look to send nonverbal messages that students should stop what they are doing and get on task without rolling eyes, snarling, or looking exasperated.

Support

Use language that indicates that you are ready to help them fix their mistake or modify their behavior, but that it is something you should figure out together; for example, "Hmmm. This does not seem to be working right now. We have made a few poor decisions. Let's start over and try again."

Of Others

Objective: To be forgiving and accepting of others.

> Jasmine is in Grade 4.
>
> Jasmine and her friends play well together, until one of Jasmine's friends starts crying and is upset about what another girl did to her. Jasmine immediately approaches you or another teacher and yells until the other child gets into trouble. When Jasmine and another student come to you with a conflict they are having on the playground, Jasmine repeats over and over that the other child pushed her.

> *Ignore*
> You listen to each of them; you tell one to play on the climbers and the other to play jump rope with other kids.
>
> *React*
> You tell each child how he/she was wrong and what he/she needs to do differently.
>
> *Respond*
> Approach the students slowly. Once they are calm, facilitate a dialogue between them. Make sure students speak to each other, not to you. Your objective in the facilitated dialogue is for each student to take ownership of what he/she did and to forgive his/her friend.

Negative feelings based on a lack of acceptance of others often arise in close relationships. The closer the relationship, the greater the expectation one has of the other.

Sometimes we expect too much from others. We are not lenient with others and do not make the same allowances for them that we might make for ourselves. We do not give others the benefit of the doubt and accept that they, too, have struggles and flaws, and are working on improving themselves. Our expectations of others can make us react in unhealthy ways when we are under stress. Students whose triggers are the unhealthy behaviors of others are constantly under stress themselves. A lack of acceptance of the weaknesses and imperfections of others often leads to negative emotions, such as anger, irritation, and frustration.

Anger is often based in a belief that unfairness is happening, that a rule has been violated, or that something is unjust. If we expect others to be capable and equal, then we will always want expectations and systems to be equivalent and fair. If a child does not understand that all students in the class are different and are able to think, feel, act, and behave as they choose, the child can become upset by the actions of others, based on their strengths or weaknesses. Note that others' strengths can be just as upsetting to a stressed student as their weaknesses: for example, a student can be annoyed that another child is a successful athlete, but also can be angry because the same child played the wrong note in music class.

Acceptance-Building Activity

Use a problem continuum to assist students in identifying the severity of the behavior of another student. Allow students to chart upsetting behavior and to evaluate how much it truly affects them. Children can be prompted:
- *Is this behavior interfering with your work?*
- *Does it hurt you?*
- *Does it change the outcome of your day?*

Students writing in their Thinking and Feeling notebooks should not be allowed to write the names of other students.

Encourage students to plot their observations on a problem continuum in their Thinking and Feeling notebooks, or use the template on page 44. Have them evaluate the level of upset that actions by another student are causing them. This is an essential step for students to take to begin to problem-solve and sort out their thinking and feeling about friendship and others in their class. Some teachers might be hesitant to attend to and acknowledge negative feelings about classmates, but students are in a small space with each other all day and they do experience a lot of conflict. It is more important and effective to provide students with appropriate avenues of expression than to shut them down and tell them not to discuss their thoughts and feelings out loud because it could hurt another child's feelings.

> ### Teacher–Class Relationship
>
> Many teachers believe they have created a classroom that views mistakes as part of the learning process, but this assumes a specific definition of the word mistake. In simple terms, "mistake" refers to an error, often an academic one. A mistake is a wrong answer given because the question is beyond the learning level of the child. These are simple mistakes that anyone could make. And these mistakes can be a legitimate part of the learning process when responded to with kindness and encouragement.
>
> But there are a lot of "mistakes" that are not as clear or easy to respond to: the behavior of a child who acts quickly without processing and planning; a child saying something that should not be said; a child acting in a way he/she should not have. Is it a mistake when a student answers questions out loud, interrupting the teacher and other students? Or when a student pushes all the paper off a desk while walking past, then looks surprised that he/she did it? We do not usually categorize this kind of behavior as a mistake. It is sometimes considered poor impulse control, but usually it is seen as a child making bad choices—to not listen, to not think before talking, to not have better control over his/her body. We judge these actions. But a mistake is an error—can't that be an error in judgment or poor calculation caused by carelessness? Did the child who pushed the papers off the desk not make an error in judgment? Was that child not careless? The behavior can be seen as just a mistake that should be accepted in a classroom, because we all make mistakes and we are a classroom that does not punish the mistakes of others.
>
> We need to examine our own classrooms and ask ourselves if we are as accepting of children who struggle and make mistakes in their behavior as we are of students who struggle and make mistakes in other areas.

The Positive Response Process

Give Feedback

Ask students to self-reflect on their behavior during disagreements. Attempt to have each student report on how they contributed to the problem instead of complaining about how the other child is at fault. Each student should be able to say what they wished they had done differently.

Set Goals

Once students have taken responsibility for what they have done, we can strive to assist them in being able to accept that a friend made a mistake and that they can forgive that friend. Model positive self-talk for students.

Regulate

Have a safe place on the playground or in the classroom for students to calm themselves before they discuss their conflicts. Paint a Calm Down bench on a playground or ask children to sit under a tree. Have an area with carpet and a pillow where children can sit and look out the window to reduce their negative energy before trying to solve a conflict.

Positive Self-Talk: *Everyone is working on something. My friend is not perfect and sometimes makes mistakes. That is okay. I can be forgiving of his/her mistakes and hope that he/she will be forgiving of mine.*

Engage

Move away from the conflict area with students so you can discuss the issue with them away from the source of their triggers. While you walk with students, don't let them tell you what the other student did wrong or continue to yell at each other.

Support

If we listen to a student complain about another child, then discipline the other student, we are creating a cycle of dependence on the teacher to reprimand and blame, which, in turn, wrecks healthy relationships. Our assistance to students needs to be in a secondary support role, so that students are not relying on the teacher's disciplinary intervention. Support students in developing the tools to deal with their own conflicts in a process that does not solve them through punishment. Ensure that your primary role on the playground is to assist students while they solve their problems in positive ways.

> **Teacher–Parent Relationship**
>
> When dealing with parents, it is important to explain to them that you do not allow students to engage you in complaints and ongoing conflicts with other students. Parents try to help their children by defending them and by advocating for them. If children struggle to get along, parents might advise their child to stay away from the other child. Sometimes we do need to intervene as adults and realize that some friendships are unhealthy for one child; however, separating children or telling children to avoid one another should not be the first step. Parents can and should encourage their children to be accepting of their friends and forgiving of them when their actions upset them. Parents can assist their children in decreasing the impact of the behavior of others as a trigger.

Of the Situation

Objective: To examine if our thinking is an accurate refection of the situation.

> Rebecca is in Grade 4. She often feels that situations are unfair.
>
> Ben and Rebecca are working together on a project. Ben does 90% of the work on his own. Rebecca is assigned a smaller task that she can manage, which represents 10% of the project. Ben helps Rebecca a little with her part of the task. At the end of the task, Rebecca complains that Ben did not help her. She claims that she did all the work and Ben hardly did anything. At first, this appears totally absurd; Ben did 90% of the work and then helped Rebecca. But it reveals the way Rebecca sees the world. Rebecca's focus is on only the section that she worked on. For that section, Ben helped out only a little, and Rebecca did do most of the work.
>
> *Ignore*
> You let it go and encourage Ben to let it go. This is how Rebecca sees the world, and you cannot change that.
>
> *React*
> You challenge Rebecca, pointing out that Ben did almost all the work on the project as a whole.

> *Respond*
> Guide Rebecca to identify her viewpoint. Show her that her perception focuses on only what she did, that she saw only her side of the problem. With her, examine Ben's point of view and Ben's thinking about the event.

Some children need a lot of assistance in evaluating if their thinking is in line with the events and information around them, if it is a true representation of their actions and those of others. Their interpretation of their actions and those of others is often biased by their negative or destructive beliefs. It is necessary for students to be able to reflect on their thinking to ensure that their point of view is realistic and is not just a result of their own negative thinking.

Support students in examining whether the beliefs they hold about themselves and others are true or false. Assist them in developing realistic viewpoints so they can better understand the social dynamics that develop around them. It is important for them to consider all the aspects, positive and negative, they bring to a situation; they have to be able to consider viewpoints that differ from their own thinking and interpretation. It is not simply about being positive and right, but about verifying beliefs, about examining the situation to determine if their thinking seems true and is a realistic representation of the events.

Individuals who are depressed often focus on, notice, and remember the negative interactions and events of the day, but do not recall the positive events.

Some people are self-critical, consistently undervaluing their strengths and their positive contributions to situations. These individuals might be very hard on themselves as they retell the details of an event. Or they might remember one negative event and neglect to mention multiple positive events. Their interpretation of and inference from the event is negatively biased against themselves and others. Over time, this affects their relationships with both themselves and others, as they struggle to deal with their critical thinking and feelings.

We will encourage students to think positively. But it is not as simple as getting students to change their negative beliefs to positive ones and be happy with themselves and others, and telling them that will build healthy relationships. It is about teaching them to verify their initial belief. They must consider their thoughts, evaluate them, and determine if their thinking matches the reality of the situation. They must come to understand that there are different ways to interpret events, and that it is these interpretations that influence how successful their social experiences are.

Acceptance-Building Activity

You can help your students revisit a situation to ascertain if there is evidence for their version of the event. Make charts with students that highlight the challenges of the school day, including possible situations and the actions of peers.

1. Use the three-column Observations and Conclusions chart on page 76 to examine negative ways of thinking and interpreting the situation, and then look at alternative explanations and ways of thinking about the situation:
   - *What He/She Said*: Have students repeat the words and dialogue exactly as they were spoken during the event.
   - *What I Heard*: Encourage students to reflect on what they thought the person meant. Have them explain their own understanding of the other person's point. You can ask them questions about how they felt and what

they thought, and use the symbols for thinking (speech balloon) and feeling (heart) to help represent their responses.

- *What He/She Could Have Meant*: Encourage students to explore alternative explanations and meanings, thinking about what the other person might have been trying to get across. Use prompts such as *I wonder if…* and *Maybe he/she was trying to…*

Positive Self-Talk: *Sometimes I need to Stop, Look, and Relisten in order to be sure I understood correctly.*

2. Discuss how our mood and outlook can change if we think about a situation in a different way.

Shapes can be used to show emotions and actions:

♡ Heart = what we feel

▭ Rectangle = what we do

🗨 Speech balloon = what we say

◯ Thought bubble = what we think

SAMPLE OBSERVATIONS AND CONCLUSIONS CHARTS

What he said.	What I heard.	What he could have meant.
it is your turn ↑ His voice made me mad (mad)	move over you are in my way (upset) wanted to hit him	It is my turn because you just had a turn (OK) I could give him a turn.

What she said	What I heard.	What she could have meant.
Where is my eraser? • She looked mad. • Sounded mad. (MAD)	You stole my eraser. (Mad)	I don't know where my eraser is and I really need it. (fine)

74 *Acceptance*

Student–Student Relationship

We can support students in interpreting and thinking about the actions and behavior of others and, in turn, how the interpretations affect their mood.

SAMPLE BEHAVIOR–MOOD CHART

Situation	Their Action	Your Thinking	Your Mood
Your friend sees you playing with someone else during recess.	Your friend snaps at you and asks your new friend to play a game she knows you hate.	Negative: *My friend is a bully*	Angry
		Alternative Explanation: *My friend feels threatened because I am playing without her and she reacted with unhealthy behavior.*	Empathetic

With proper examination of this interaction, students can begin to understand the reasons behind the actions of others.

Teacher–Teacher Relationship

The different ways of thinking about the same event can lead to very different moods and behaviors for yourself.

SAMPLE BEHAVIOR–MOOD CHART

Situation	Their Actions	Your Thinking	Your Mood
You are collaborating with a colleague.	Every time you try to speak or add something, he interrupts you and paraphrases what you say.	Negative: • *He is rude.* • *He does not think I have anything to contribute.*	Irritated Offended
		Alternative Explanation: *He interrupts when he gets excited.*	Sympathetic

The Positive Response Process

Give Feedback

Draw attention to the details of the situation that students are focused on and are using to draw their inferences and interpretations. You might need to explicitly tell students that their thinking about events tends to be shaped by negative thinking: "I think that we missed some of the positive details of this situation and we homed in on the negative sides of it."

Observations and Conclusions

What He/She Said	What I Heard	What He/She Could Have Meant

Set Goals

Students need to question if there is another side to the story and if they are using all available information to draw their conclusions and make assumptions. They have to learn to examine alternative ways of thinking to form different perspectives.

Regulate

To help students self-regulate, have calming exercises posted on the wall.

If a student is loudly complaining about an issue, signal to the student to pause first. Ask the student to use his/her energy to go to the hallway and do five minutes of stretching poses. Tell the student that you have to finish up with one student and that you will be available for him/her when he/she has finished the stretches.

Engage

Approach the student slowly and deliberately. Smile and ask him/her how his/her body feels after taking a few minutes to release the negative energy. Listen to the student and ensure that you are attentive to his/her explanation of the problem. It is important for students to be given a voice and to be heard.

Support

Ask students to come up with one possible alternative explanation for the situation that is upsetting them or making them angry. Ask them if it was their friend who was upset about this event; ask what might be one thing they would say to try to give a different point of view.

Of the Thinking of Others

We are able to sustain our relationships only if we are constantly able to take into account the thoughts and feelings of others.

Objective: To consider what another person might be thinking and how it influences their actions and behavior.

> Sadie is in Grade 5. She is hypersensitive and always infers the negative in social interactions.
>
> Sadie is often bothered and upset about something. You have observed her many times in group work, working well with others until, for some reason unclear to you, she stomps off or shuts down. She then wanders around the classroom, talking under her breath. She can often be seen whispering to other girls in the class. Then the group of girls can be observed excluding another child, even confronting the other child and accusing her of doing something to Sadie.
>
> *Ignore*
> You sit with the group of girls and remind them about the classroom code of conduct: "In this room we are kind and friendly to everyone."
>
> *React*
> You tell Sadie that excluding is a form of bullying and that she has to stop being mean.
>
> *Respond*
> Understand that there is a lot more going on in this situation than Sadie simply bullying other children. Sit with the group to observe their dynamic and to try to piece together what is going on.

Positive Self-Talk: *My friend might have a different side of the story. I think I need to figure out more about this situation by considering what my friend is thinking.*

In order to build healthy relationships and create a positive classroom community, we need to help students understand that other students in the class think differently from themselves, that they have different ways of thinking and interpreting events, and that their perspectives matter.

The ability to think about the perspective of others and to consider another point of view helps children better manage challenges that arise each day. To look at events from multiple angles and to be able to understand that there are indeed many sides to every story reduces stressful experiences. Without the ability to stop and analyze the other person's viewpoint, there can be great confusion and misunderstanding in a child's relationships and interpersonal dynamics. Stress can arise because the bias in the interpretation of events makes the child truly unable to understand why another person behaves in a particular way.

Some students easily accept that other students hold different interpretations, needs, and wants in situations. They exert less energy trying to prove that they are right or that the other person has misunderstood something. Students who can accept that others might hold entirely different ideas, thoughts, and beliefs are more easily able to accept interactions that require that students compromise and work together. For students who are unable to accept that others hold different thoughts and feelings, these situations act as triggers, upsetting them and beginning a cycle of distress.

Student–Class Relationship

If the trigger that causes students stress is that someone else holds a different opinion, they will try to get everyone to agree with them or state that they are right. When they do not succeed, they can become upset and focused on the idea that someone else will not change his/her opinion to match theirs. These students struggle because they believe that they can change the thinking and opinions of others. We can support these students by emphasizing that others hold ideas and opinions of their own, that we can inquire about those ideas and learn from them, but that our primary goal should not be to try to change them.

Schoolwide Relationship

If we teach all students in the school the same social problem-solving techniques, over time, students will be able to apply conflict-resolution strategies during social interactions to reduce the development of conflicts. This paradigm requires multiple staff members committed to the same system so that, year after year and classroom after classroom, students are exposed to the same procedure while they resolve their conflicts.

Acceptance-Building Activity

Conflict-resolution mediation is an effective way to facilitate student problem-solving. Mediators must understand that their role is not simply to solve the problem in the moment. The mediator's role is to facilitate discussion and conflict resolution. Their goal is to put systems in place that will prevent future misunderstandings, negative feelings, and similar situations. The mediator is involved

to make sure that students are talking to each other; that the students are following the dialogue expectations (see Conflict Resolution Checklist on page 82).
- Mediators can intervene to prompt students to use a softer voice, to slow down, to use kind words, to try to relax the muscles in their faces, or to speak only about issues that occurred that day, not in the past.
- Mediators can support the students by paraphrasing for them when they have trouble expressing themselves:
  - "You meant to say, Layla, 'It upsets me when you tell me that I can't play with Sheila.'"
  - "Could you try repeating your sentence with something that sounds more similar to this, 'Rob, you have the right to your ideas, but it is not fair that you try to make me play your way'?"
  - "You can say the same thing with kinder words. For example, you could say, 'When you spread rumors about me, it is very upsetting. People were really mad at me and some people stopped being my friend. I have been very confused all month and I did not want to go to school. What you said about me is the reason I have felt depressed and miserable. Your actions had a huge impact on the way I felt.'"
- Mediators can support students nonverbally: for example, by taking a big deep breath to show how to self-soothe and slow down the process; by gently waving their hands to show that everyone needs to slow down and calm down before proceeding; by pointing to indicate that the students should look at each other, not at the mediator.

1. The first priority for a mediator is to calm the students involved in the conflict. It is hard to solve conflict while you are upset. Mediators must first support the students in calming down, relaxing, and decreasing the negative effects of the conflict. The mediators need to support a regulation process in which the students involved stop what they are doing (see pages 51 and 97 for more on Stop). Here are some options:
   - Breathe slowly ten times.
   - Close your eyes.
   - Close your eyes and imagine something that makes you happy.
   - Read a joke book for a minute.
   - Look out the window.
   - Do an exercise activity.
   - Pick a few yoga poses or exercises from the picture wall and do them.
   - Color in a picture.
   - Get a drink of water.

   Having students add their own visuals to the Stop list (page 82) can be helpful in helping them pick their favorite self-calming strategies.

SAMPLE OF STOP LIST OF SELF-CALMING STRATEGIES

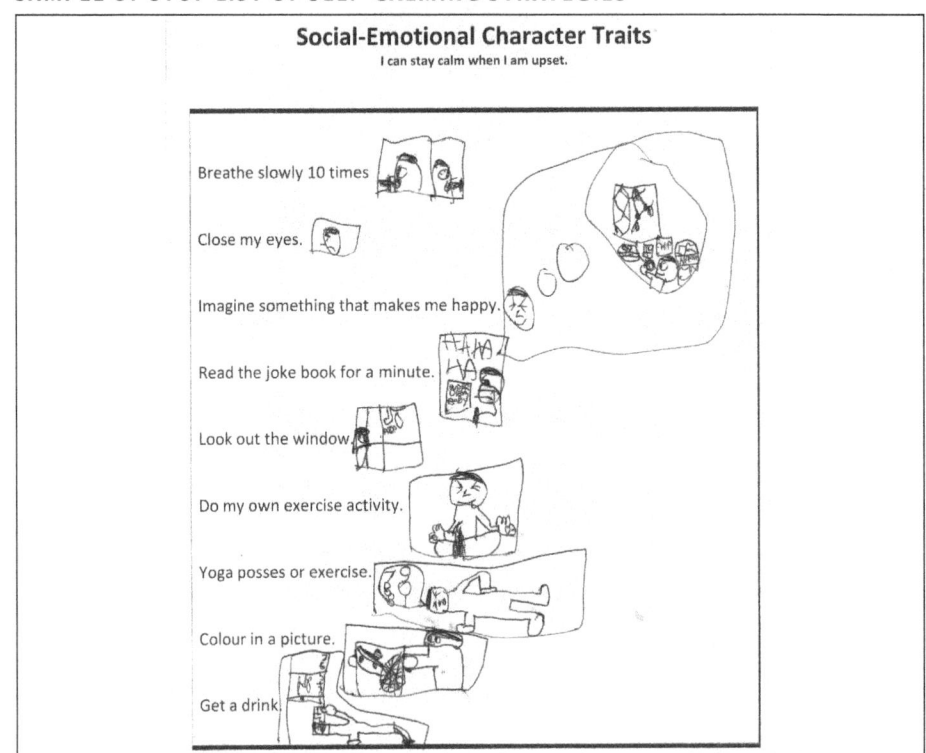

Social-Emotional Character Traits
I can stay calm when I am upset.

- Breathe slowly 10 times
- Close my eyes.
- Imagine something that makes me happy.
- Read the joke book for a minute.
- Look out the window.
- Do my own exercise activity.
- Yoga posses or exercise.
- Colour in a picture.
- Get a drink.

2. Once the students have taken a short break, they answer questions on the Ready for Mediation form on page 83 to see if they are ready to speak to each other with respect, kindness, and gentleness.
3. Using the Conflict Resolution recording sheet on page 84, each student completes his/her own Situation/Action/Thinking forms before the discussion starts.
4. At this point, students speak to each other and express what they are want, need, think, and feel. You might need to remind students to speak to each other, not to the mediator. The students can show each other their Situation/Action/Thinking sheets and examine them to determine if there were any misunderstandings.
5. As each student expresses what he/she needs, they both record it on the Want/Need section of their Conflict Resolution sheets.
6. As each student expresses what he/she is sorry for, they both record it on the Sorry section of their Conflict Resolution sheets.
7. As each student expresses what he/she wishes he/she had done differently, they both record it on the Wish section of their Conflict Resolution sheets.
8. Students discuss and decide whether there were two different perspectives on the situation; the answer is recorded on their Conflict Resolution sheets.
9. The mediator encourages students to think of negative reactions to the conflict that would make the problem bigger; they are recorded.
10. The mediator encourages students to think of positive reactions to the conflict that would make the problem smaller or make it go away; they are recorded.
11. Each student gives one alternative action they can use the next time to try to avoid conflict; they are recorded.

> ### Student–Student Relationship
>
> Peer-to-peer mediation is an effective way of facilitating student problem-solving. Teachers do not have the time day-to-day to facilitate social problem-solving as much as students require it, so this process builds in extra helpers. Students gain exposure to conflict resolution strategies in their classes and come to act as mediators. Whenever and wherever possible, the mediators should be students involved in conflict themselves, not simply those with strong social-emotional character traits who are rarely involved in conflict. Students who are often involved in conflict can gain insight and perspective by being the mentors. While this requires teaching and supervision, you can set up a mentoring situation in which a more-experienced mediator trains a new one.

The Positive Response Process

Give Feedback

Directly explain to students the need to think about their classmates as individuals who have their own thoughts and needs, feelings of happiness and sadness: "The other students in the class are people too, with ideas and thoughts and feelings of their own. They each have good and bad days of their own, sometimes crying and feeling sad, embarrassed, or guilty about things that happened at school."

Set Goals

Encourage students to set a daily goal of taking a minute to look at the student sitting beside them and to consider what their peer might be thinking and feeling.

Regulate

When children are yelling at each other and dysregulated, encourage them to consider what another student is thinking and feeling on the inside. Remind them that, as we sort this problem out, we want to use a soft tone of voice that does not make another feel bad.

Engage

Sit with the students, ensuring that they are facing each other and that you are slightly behind them. In this position, they have to engage with each other, not you, while discussing the conflict and how it makes them feel.

Support

Strive to create a dynamic in which children want to speak with each other, instead of to you, to solve their problems. Their independence will increase if your facilitation places the responsibility on them to speak to each other and to problem-solve in a systematic way, so that they do not rely on you for conflict resolution.

Conflict Resolution Checklist

Language must be   ☐ kind

Voice must be   ☐ soft
                            ☐ slow

Face must be   ☐ gentle
                            ☐ soft

Words must be   ☐ polite
                            ☐ kind
                            ☐ friendly

Explanation must be   ☐ on topic
                                        ☐ about today, not other days

Stop

I can stay calm when I am upset.

Name: _____

Breathe slowly 10 times.

Close my eyes.

Imagine something that makes me happy.

Read a joke book for a minute.

Look out the window.

Do my own exercise activity.

Do yoga poses or exercise.

Color in a picture.

Get a drink of water.

Ready for Mediation

Name: _____

Date: _____

Mediator: _____

Other student involved: _____

Since our bodies were
- ☐ agitated
- ☐ restless
- ☐ fidgety
- ☐ energized
- ☐ other: _____

we thought that we would calm our bodies down so that we were ready to talk calmly, softly, with kind voices. We decided that we would

_____

I agree to the following conditions:
- ☐ Once we are feeling calm and less upset, we will sit down to discuss our problem.
- ☐ I am ready to use a soft and gentle voice.
- ☐ If I begin to get upset, I can ask for a break so that I don't say something I will regret.
- ☐ I am ready to examine this problem from my point of view and to express what I need, want, think, and feel.
- ☐ I am ready to examine this problem from the other person's point of view and to consider what he/she needs, wants, thinks, and feels.

Conflict Resolution

Situation/Action/Thinking

Situation	My Actions	My Friend's Thinking	Alternative Explanation

Situation	My Friend's Actions	My Thinking	Alternative Explanation

Want/Need

_____ wants/needs _____.
_____ wants/needs _____.
_____ wants/needs _____.

Sorry

_____ is sorry that he/she _____.
_____ is sorry that he/she _____.
_____ is sorry that he/she _____.

Wish

_____ wishes he/she had _____.
_____ wishes he/she had _____.
_____ wishes he/she had _____.

Were there two perspectives to this situation? ☐ Yes ☐ No

Provide a negative way to solve this problem:

_____

Provide a positive way to solve this problem:

_____

Next time, _____ will try to _____.

Next time, _____ will try to _____.

Of the Need to Adapt

Objective: To be willing to adapt our behavior because of the needs of others and to reduce their triggers.

> Zoe is in Grade 5.
>
> Zoe is a bright and creative child. She is a group leader and an expert in many areas. However, working with Zoe means doing everything Zoe's way. She will lead the group, but she does so by making all the decisions.
>
> *Ignore*
> You feel it is good for children to work out this type of challenge. The other students can either go along with her leadership or they can figure it out.
>
> *React*
> You instruct Zoe and the other students that this is a group project and it will be accepted only if they are able to work together as a group.
>
> *Respond*
> Understand that Zoe struggles with inflexibility, an area of weakness for her. With your support, she can learn to consider the ideas and needs of her peers and to incorporate them into group work. Plan ahead with Zoe by giving her clear choice of some things she will need to be flexible about, decisions she will have to let other students vote for; for example, make it clear to Zoe that the group will be deciding the country that will be the subject of their research project. The group will vote and she will need to go along with whatever decision the group makes. Make it clear to her that "going along with it" means that she must smile at the group members and make an accepting statement about their decision.

When space is being shared with others, there will be disagreements and challenging moments. Students who are flexible enough to compromise and adapt their behavior will experience less stress and adversity in their daily lives, because they will have to deal with less reactive behavior from other people. Students who are able to alter their behavior to the needs of a group or the situation without it negatively affecting them contribute to a positive cycle of actions and behavior. These students tend to be flexible thinkers. They might want something ("I want to play tag") but, if the other students want to play soccer, they adapt what they want to go along with the activity of the group. They experience flexible thinking: e.g., "I wanted to play tag, but no one else does. If I want to have fun at recess, I can play the game that everyone else is playing." Flexible thinking allows students to change their behavior and go along with the group.

Rigid thinkers get stuck on a need. They think that something needs to be done in a particular way, that there is one thing that they must have, or that a rule must be followed. They might need to play a certain game, not be able to go out for recess early, or have to have a certain object in hand or a ritual done in a precise way. These children experience many hard moments in the day because their thinking gets them stuck and they become increasingly fixated on a belief that they need to have something in particular. As their stress increases, their belief in their need increases.

With your students, examine the impact of actions on the group. Let students see the link between a change in their behavior and the way other students feel about them and respond to them. Explain to students that they have the right to act as they want, but if it upsets other students in the classroom, the other students will have upset feelings of their own.

> ### Teacher–Self Relationship
>
> We can get stuck in the same thinking as students do. For example, you are asked to stay late after school for an unplanned meeting. You don't want to do it; you want to say, "No." You have two choices—to agree or to disagree. The way you ultimately feel about this decision will be based on what you think after the fact. If you agree to stay after school and are able to understand the reasons why you did and stop thinking about it, you will feel okay with the decision. If you stay, but then start to think about all the reasons that you should not have done it, you will be angry about your decision. It is not necessarily about the decisions we make; it is our ability to make a decision and then stop thinking about it repeatedly that will determine if we end up being upset after the decision.

Acceptance-Building Activity

Derived from Social Thinking, this process is called Behavior Mapping (Winner, 2010). It tracks the impact of one's actions on the feelings and actions of others. It helps students understand the link between their challenging behavior and how others feel and act.

1. With students, create a chart with four titles: *Your Actions*, *Feelings of Group Members*, *Actions of Group Members*, and *Your Feelings*.
   - Under *Your Actions*, students describe the action (the behavior or words they used) that got them into a challenging situation.
   - Have students complete the *Feelings of Group Members* column by considering how their actions or words would make the members of their group feel. With younger students, you can give them a choice of emotions: e.g., *Happy*, *Mad*, *Nervous*, or *Sad*.
   - In the *Feelings of Group Members* section, students explain the behavior or words of other people in response to their action.
   - In the final column, *Your Feelings*, students reflect on their feelings at the end of the interaction.

SAMPLE BEHAVIOR TRACKING CHART

Your Actions	Feelings of Group Members	Actions of Group Members	Your Feelings
You decide everything for your group and do not listen to the ideas of anyone else.	They feel upset and left out. Maybe they think that you do not respect them or value their contributions.	Group members begin to yell at you and walk away.	You might feel sad.

Positive Self-Talk: *If I do only what I want, then I am not thinking about the thoughts and feelings of my friend.*

2. Help students understand the link between a change in their behavior and how others feel and act.

Your Actions	Feelings of Group Members	Action of Group Members	Your Feelings
You accept the ideas of your group.	They feel happy. They think that you respect them and want their opinions.	They listen to you and say kind things to you.	You feel included and happy.

Student–Self Relationship

Being willing to alter one's behavior to suit the thoughts and needs of others does not mean allowing yourself to be taken advantage of. Chart explicitly with students tangible examples of what we can compromise about and what we should not. They need to understand that, when we ask them to be flexible and willing to change their behavior to make someone else happy, we never mean that they should allow themselves to be hurt or treated unfairly.

SAMPLE COMPROMISE CHART

It is worth compromising and going along with the group when…	It is not worth going along with the group when…
- Most people in the group agree with an idea or a project. - We are trying to figure out what game to play. - It lets us keep working on a project. - It is a level 1–5 problem (Not a problem–A little problem) on the Problem Continuum (see page 44).	- Someone is being hurt. - Someone is being left out. - Someone is using unkind words. - Someone is telling you to do something dangerous.

Students must begin to understand that they have choices to make all day long. Even if they think that they cannot control their actions and feel dysregulated, they can slow down their reactions and make decisions in the moment to avoid unhealthy behaviors.

The Positive Response Process

Give Feedback

Have students evaluate their behavior and the subsequent feelings and behaviors of other students in the classroom. For example, a student might say, "When I told everyone in the group that I am the leader and we have to do the project my way, they looked upset. Then they stood up and walked away."

Set Goals

We must assist students in understanding that they need to consider the negative implications of their behavior. They need to be willing to alter their behavior to meet the needs of people they share space and interact with.

Regulate

Encourage students to perform one self-calming activity—e.g., going for a walk, getting a drink of water from the hallway. Allow students a mental break before trying to alter their behavior. When the student comes back from the hallway, meet him/her at the door before he/she rejoins the group.

Engage

Be available to hear the student's thinking and needs. Don't cut off a student while he/she is talking and trying to sort out feelings. Let students know that you believe in them; for example, "I see that you are trying to be flexible and to accept the ideas of your friends. That is a huge first step. Can you use the time here with me to think of one idea of your group members that you could accept and work with?"

Support

When students do change their behavior for others, be attentive to the fact that it is very hard on them. They might be extra-sensitive after the fact and need more space than usual after compromising. Because their stress level is heightened, they might be more reactive for the rest of the day and get upset about something that they could typically handle. If possible, try to give a student who has altered his/her behavior a little space throughout that day. Recognize that the child exhibited huge success in an accomplishment and it required a lot of energy and control over his/her thinking.

If you want to support and help teach a child to be more flexible through this approach, it will take years. You, his/her parents, and other teachers will need to support this child in learning to relinquish some of his/her fixations through slow and deliberate compromising. You will not witness success at the speed you would like, since the gains will be very small and will occur over time. But each time an inflexible student compromises, it is a huge success to be celebrated: "Wow, amazing! You took control of your thinking. You did not get stuck in the one idea. You were able to try a new way. Well done." See page 89 for the Behavior Tracking template: students can fill it out and take it home to explain their successful interaction to parents.

SAMPLE BEHAVIOR TRACKING

Shapes can be used to show emotions and actions:

♥ Heart = what we feel

▭ Rectangle = what we do

🗨 Speech balloon = what we say

◯ Thought bubble = what we think

Behavior Tracking

Track the impact of your behavior.

Name: _____

Draw pictures to tell your success story! You changed your behavior to make a friend feel good.

The action I wanted to do:	But it would have made my friend feel… ♡
Instead I…	This made my friend feel… ♡

Pembroke Publishers ©2014 *Stop the Stress in Schools* by Joey Mandel ISBN 978-1-55138-298-2

Of the Behavior of Others

Objective: To accept that sometimes others around us will be unable to alter their behavior, even to meet our needs.

Chase is in Grade 6.

Chase and Brandon share a locker. They argue every day about the state of the locker. Brandon is organized and neat, while Chase struggles to keep his belongings together and his stuff in order. In an ideal situation, Chase would have his own locker, but there are not enough lockers to go around. Chase and Brandon must share this space.

Ignore
You do nothing. You figure that, over the course of the year, they will each help each other sort this problem out.

React
You tell Chase that it is unacceptable that his locker is disorganized and that he will miss every recess until it is cleaned up.

Respond
Explain to the boys together that the situation they are in is very hard on both of them, because they are sharing space and for each there is a different way of keeping the space that makes them happy. Be available to them and assist them while they work through a way to be able to share the tiny space.

We cannot control the outcome of all events. Some students place a great deal of importance and focus on fairness and rules. They exert a lot of mental energy ensuring that things happen in a particular manner. The greater a child's core belief that things should always be fair and follow a particular pattern of logic and justice is, the more often that child will be upset as things do not work out the way he/she believes they should. It leaves such students thinking that the school, the teacher, and the other students are unfair and perhaps against them.

It is important to be able to assist children in accepting that things will not always work out their way, even when they are, in fact, correct and right. People unable to accept this fundamental truth will consistently struggle with not getting their own—i.e., the right—way.

For some students, a violation of their sense of fairness acts as a significant trigger. These students struggle in school, trying to alter the behavior and actions of classmates. They might believe, "If I am right, then he/she has to change his/her behavior." A student who holds this belief will have daily struggles, trying to get another person to interact in a way that he/she wants or expects them to. If the children in your class always think that everything should be exactly fair, they will constantly be faced with situations that offend their beliefs and upset them. They will be stressed by the unfairness of situations.

Positive Self-Talk: *This is what my friend needs to do right now. This is what she needs to do to make it through the day, so I will try my best to be okay with it, even if I don't think it is fair.*

Student-Class Relationship

A teacher who believes that he/she is right and that students have to change their behavior to suit his/her needs and expectations will struggle constantly with his/her class. His/her stress levels will be consistently high.

Some students are not yet at a stage at which they are able to change their behavior, even when what they are doing upsets another student. As a result, such students consistently upset other students. Teachers must work hard to manage the negative thinking of the classmates of these students, so they can change their expectations of the student's behavior without being upset or thinking badly of the student.

Acceptance-Building Activity

1. Discuss with students that we have control over our own behavior; we can control the way we act, think, and feel. But we do not have control over the behavior of others; we cannot control the way others act, think, or feel.
2. Brainstorm with students what they can and can't control. Make a chart with students that shows what they can and can't control.

CONTROL CHART

I CAN'T...	I CAN...
• change how someone else thinks • control someone else's actions	• change how I think • control my own actions

3. Using a typical playground problem, ask students to brainstorm concrete examples of what they can and can't control.

SAMPLE CONTROL CHART

Someone keeps yelling and screaming during recess.	
I CAN'T...	I CAN...
• make the student stop yelling • force the student to be quiet	• go somewhere else • tell myself that it is not that big a deal • distract myself

4. Using the Change: Drawing chart (page 93) or Change: Writing chart (page 94), have students create a drawing or narrative that includes two ways of handling a challenging situation in which someone else is upsetting them: one in which the student focuses on the behavior of others; the other in which the student focuses on his/her own behavior, thoughts, and feelings.
5. Encourage students to rate the size of the problem for each approach.

The Positive Response Process

Give Feedback

Trace with students the impact of focusing on the upsetting behavior of others: for example, "You continue to be upset at your classmates for something they do every day. You know that it would be great if they did not do that and I am trying to help them manage their behavior. But for now, they have not been able to stop it. You are losing out too, because you are getting upset every day about something you have no control over. The only thing that you have control over is how upset you get. You have control over how upset their behavior makes you."

Set Goals

Encourage students to set personal goals for themselves to manage their strong emotions instead of focusing on the behavior of others. Goals include focusing on what they can do to improve the situation, identifying any aspect of the situation over which they have control, and determining what they themselves can do to make the situation less upsetting. This might involve walking away from someone who is bothering them; using self-talk to tell themselves that the situation is not a big problem; or focusing on good aspects of someone else's personality. This puts students' energy into something more productive than trying to change the behavior of others.

Regulate

When a child is distraught about the actions of another child, instead of problem-solving the issue, focus on calming activities to minimize how upset all students get. If the student appears too upset to problem-solve or participate in a discussion, encourage him/her to use a self-calming strategy; for example, have the student look out the window or close his/her eyes and count backward from 20. It is best not to begin a problem-solving conversation unless students are at a low or medium level of stress.

Engage

Approach the students who are upset with each other. Smile at each of them and encourage them to smile at each other. Just smiling can help get positive energy into the dynamic!

Support

Have each student begin by saying something positive about the other. Then ask them to reflect on their goals and to consider ways that they can solve the problem by changing their own behavior, not by telling another person what to do differently.

Change: Drawing

I can't change others; I can only change myself.

Name: _____   Date: _____

Describe a situation in which some is upsetting you. Please do not use real names of students in our class.

Situation:	
I CAN'T…	**I CAN…**
Draw a picture of what would happen if you focus on the behavior of the other person.	Draw a picture of what would happen if you focused on your own behavior.

How big is the problem if you focus on the behavior of the other person? Mark it on this scale.

1   5   10

_____

How big is the problem if you focus on your own behavior? Mark it on this scale.

1   5   10

_____

Change: Writing

I can't change others; I can only change myself.

Name: _____ Date: _____

Describe a situation in which some is upsetting you. Please do not use real names of students in our class.

Situation:	
I CAN'T…	**I CAN…**
Brainstorm what would happen if you focus on the behavior of the other person.	Brainstorm what would happen if you focused on your own behavior.
Characters:	Characters:
Setting:	Setting:
Problem:	Problem:
The behavior of the other person:	My behavior:

How big is the problem if you focus on the behavior of the other person? Mark it on this scale.

1   5   10

How big is the problem if you focus on your own behavior? Mark it on this scale.

1   5   10

Pick one of the stories and write about it.

5

Ability to Manage Stress

It is great to be aware of our challenges and to accept them, but if we stop at that, we might not push ourselves to face what challenges us. The motivation and ability to face a challenge, to expose ourselves to it, to attempt to use our strategies and tools, to fail and then try again are the skills that will allow us to manage stress. If we avoid challenges or use maladaptive ways of coping, we perpetuate a cycle of stress. It is only by facing challenges that we can decrease this cycle of negative actions, thoughts, and feelings. In this chapter, we will examine the ability to

- self-calm
- change the way we think
- change the way others feel
- go back and try again
- apply stress-reduction strategies

Self-Calming

Objective: To understand that we can change the way we feel physically with calming strategies.

> Liam is in Grade 3. He struggles with time anxiety.
>
> Liam worries about the pressure of time. In class, his face goes white and he becomes agitated any time the pace of the class begins to pick up. He starts asking a lot of questions and indicates that he is unsure if he will be able to complete his work; he complains that there is not enough time.
>
> *Ignore*
> You encourage Liam to get as much work done as he can in the time he has and not to worry.
>
> *React*
> You tell Liam that he is wasting time by asking so many questions. You indicate that if he actually did the work, he would be done.
>
> *Respond*
> Approach Liam slowly and calmly. Take a blank piece of paper to cover the parts of the assignment he does not need to worry about to begin; highlight the section he should try to focus on. Encourage his efforts to self-calm: "I liked it when you took a break to calm yourself down in that situation. I wonder if we can apply that strategy to other times."

Exposure to any stress trigger releases negative biochemicals in our bodies and increases negative tension. Since stress triggers have this physiological effect, it is important to teach children physical tools for self-calming. Once the Fight, Flight, or Freeze state has triggered the body's negative physical response—making it jittery, jumpy, tight, tense, or frozen—we must support children physically to bring them back to a calmer state. If they stay in a place where they are experiencing negative tension, they might continue to move up the stress curve (see page 8) into higher and higher states of stress.

We can take control of the physical impact of stress by engaging in positive sensory and relaxation activities to calm our tensions and release positive biochemicals through our bodies. If we systematically model engaging in sensory, breathing, and visualization activities, we can teach children that they can control their bodies. They will learn that they have the power to change their body's reaction to stress by applying what they learn.

Always prioritize calming the child first.

Teachers typically approach children in challenging situations. We have excellent ideas about what we think they should do to calm down and solve the problem. During high stress, children enter the Fight, Flight, or Freeze state, in which they cannot access their words or process your verbal instructions. We need to practice self-calming before students actually find themselves in high-stress situations. Knowing that the student will not behave rationally and logically, we must focus on physical ways to calm him/her.

Student–Self Relationship

Before any problem-solving or any discussion, support children in making sure that their bodies are calm. Help them see exactly what that looks like. List or draw with students on chart paper or the interactive whiteboard exactly what it looks like to stop and calm down.

SAMPLE OF STOP AND CALM DOWN CHART

Looks Like	Does Not Look Like
Feet planted on the ground	Walking toward the problem
Wiggling my feet in my shoes so that I can feel them	Moving around, being unfocused
Hands in my pockets	Waving my hands at a person or the problem
Mouth closed	Talking or screaming to prove my point
Eyes looking down at my feet, to concentrate on grounding myself	Eyes glaring at the person I am upset with
Eyes closed so that I am not focused on the problem	Eyes looking at the teacher for him/her to fix the problem
Eyes looking up at the trees because they help calm me	Eyes focused on my trigger
Eyes looking out the window because it helps calm me	Eyes watching the other kids in the class to see if they are judging me
Taking slow, deep breaths to relax my body	Holding my breath

Ability-Building Activities

There are four basic steps in supporting physical self-calming:
- Grounding: *Stop moving, plant your feet, and sit down.*
- Breathing: *Take in long slow breaths.*
- Visualizing: *Imagine something that makes you happy and tell yourself you can calm yourself down.*
- Noticing: *Observe how your body experiences relaxation.*(Melrose, 2013)

These steps can be taught and practiced at times when students are not stressed and upset. They can be part of the morning routine and repeated during transition times throughout the day. As students become proficient at sensory self-calming, you can begin to apply the technique just before known triggers, during conflict resolution and during moments of medium stress.

Grounding Activity: STOP

The point of grounding is to support students in ceasing to move, talk, or try to explain or defend themselves, as these behaviors increase agitation and increase stress:
- *Stop moving and stop talking.*
- *Plant your feet on the ground.*
- *Put your hands at your sides.*
- *Look away from the problem: look up at the sky, look down at your feet, or turn away.*

Breathing Activity: Deep Breathing

1. Explain deep belly breathing.
2. Have students find a place where they are comfortable: standing up, on the ground, sitting in a chair, walking around. Tell students to find a position that is comfortable for them.
3. You can model the breathing technique, but encourage students to breathe at their own pace. Have students close their eyes and follow your lead.
    - *Stop.*
    - *Breathe in slowly. Breathe out slowly.*
    - *Take slow, deep breaths, filling your lungs with air.*
    - *Blow out long, full breaths; raise your hands if it helps.*
    - *Imagine it's your birthday:* "I can take a slow, deep breath. I will smell the chocolate cake"; *and* "I can let out a big, long breath. I will blow out all the candles."
    - *Repeat.*

Visualizing Activity: Happy Boxes

It is difficult for children to visualize, especially when they are dysregulated. To support them in the process of visualization, begin the process with concrete materials. A Happy Box contains physical things or images of things that make the child happy.

1. Have students bring in small objects (e.g., erasers, small toys, rocks and shells) and pictures (e.g., of their family or a place they love) to put in their Happy Boxes. They can draw things that make them happy (e.g., a favorite animal) to include.

You might let students place a piece of paper, a toy, an eraser, etc. on their stomachs to observe how it rises and falls.

Buy cute boxes from the dollar store, or have each students bring in a small, simple box. Have students decorate their boxes with colors, designs, and stickers.

Self-Calming 97

2. Model the process of self-calming. Pick up, say, a bunny and smile at it. Rub the bunny with your hand and smile. Verbally link the action to a relaxed feeling: "This helps me feel softer and calmer inside."
3. Guide students through the process of visualization:
   - *Pick up your Happy Box.*
   - *Find a quiet spot in the room and settle in it (e.g., lie on the carpet, sit in your seat). Close your eyes.*
   - *Think about the objects in your Happy Box. In your mind, choose an object you think will help calm you down.*
   - *Now open your box and retrieve the object you believe will help you self-calm.*
   - *Now that you are holding your object, close your eyes and picture it in your mind: its size, its color, its shape.*
   - *Push your feet into the floor. Breathe in slowly. Keep picturing the object you are holding in your hands.*
4. Repeated use of Happy Boxes will teach students to link the objects in them with an image in their head of something happy and with the feeling of calm.

Noticing Activity

1. To support students in noticing their internal sensations, begin by supporting their noticing of external sensations: *Today we will be working on mindfulness, to help us pay more attention to what is going on around us and to our senses.*
2. Pass a raisin to each student. Tell them not to eat the raisins.
3. Guide students through noticing details of the raisin:
   - *Hold it in your hand.*
   - *Close your eyes and really feel it in your hand. Feel how heavy it is and where it is on your palm.*
   - *Take your other hand and touch it. How does it feel?*
   - *Bring it up to your nose and smell it.*
   - *Open your eyes and look at it. What color is it? What does it look like? How many ridges does it have?*
   - *If you are daring, lick it once. What does it taste like?*
   - *Now tear it in half. What does it feel like to tear it?*
   - *Eat one half. What does it taste like?*
4. Discuss with students the process of noticing the raisins:
   - *Have you ever taken this long to eat a raisin? Have you ever really looked at it, imagined it, pictured it, touched it, examined it, and smelled it? Or do you eat twenty of them at the same time? Why is it good to slow down and focus on the raisin?*
   - *Ask yourself, "If can focus this long and hard on a raisin, could I also begin to focus this long and hard on my actions, thoughts, or feelings? Could I begin to notice the way I act, think, and feel?"*
5. Using the Noticing charts on pages 100 and 101, let students begin to explore and notice their actions, thoughts, and feelings at various times during the day. The first handout examines a student's actions, thoughts, and feelings during one activity; this allows them to focus on one their reactions to one subject. The second handout allows students to see the variation throughout the day; it can be used without the expectation of completing the entire chart.

Take your time here. Don't rush the time between thinking about what is inside the box and opening the box to retrieve the object. Use this time to have students imagine, think, picture, or visualize something without seeing it or touching it.

Positive Self-Talk: *I have the ability. I can move from feeling stressed to feeling relaxed if I use my self-calming strategies.*

The Positive Response Process

Give Feedback

Let students understand that, without meaning to, they increase the panic and negative tension in their bodies when they are upset. If they are able to identify negative feelings when they experience distress, they can begin to control the amount that stress affects them.

Set Goal

Students must learn their stress curve (see pages 8 and 45) and know when they can take active, positive steps to control the impact that stress has on them. They need to understand that they have the power to change the way they feel.

Regulate

Some children in an extreme state of Fight, Flight, or Freeze become unable to stop and move away from the trigger and out of the situation. They are not ready to begin self-calming, and suggesting calming techniques would only increase their stress level. For students who experience these intense states, a first step in self-calming is being willing to move out of the space of the trigger. Any form of break they can take—in distance, with time away—might be their first action in controlling their behavior when they are under stress.

Engage

Draw the stress curve with students. Stand with a student while he/she identifies the level of stress he/she feels.

> A study with Ontario students indicated that a safe space in their school environment where they could go when experiencing stress was the single most important thing that schools could offer students to support their mental health needs.

> On this stress curve, the student identifies the strategy he could use when he moves into high stress.

SAMPLE STRESS CURVE

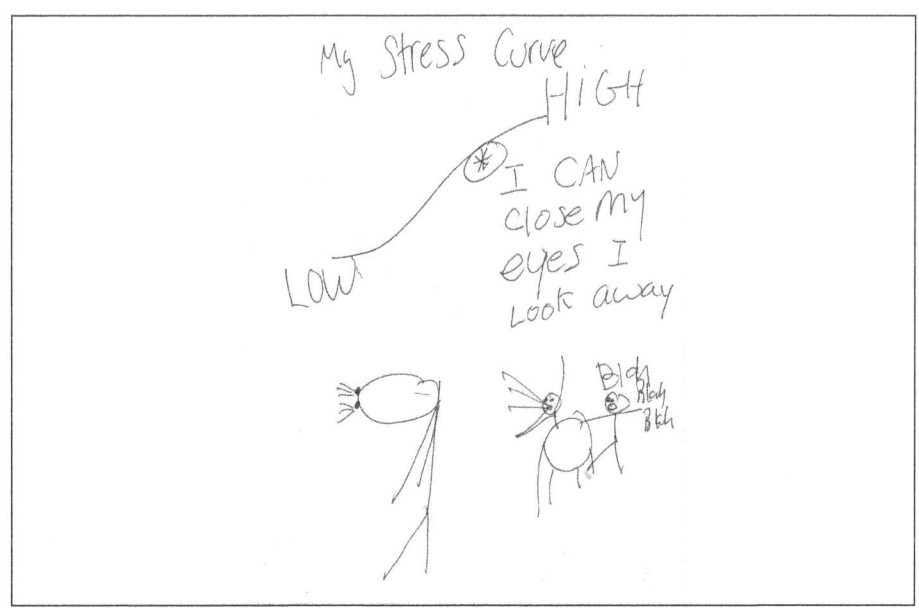

Support

Be willing to attend to students while they calm themselves. When you are done, self-talk the positive effects of taking the time to release tension. Explain that your shoulders feel lighter, your inside voice is not talking as much, and your mind is clearer.

Noticing During an Activity

I can notice how I act, think, and feel.

Name: _____

Describe how you acted, what you thought, and how you felt during an activity.

Subject	Act	Think	Feel

Noticing through the Day

I can notice how I act, think, and feel.

Name: _____

Describe how you acted, what you thought, and how you felt during an activity.

Subject	Act	Think	Feel
Guided Reading			
Recess			
Gym			
Lunch			
Math			
Recess			
Science			

Changing the Way We Think

Objective: To understand that we can change the way we think by using positive thinking strategies.

> Avery is in Grade 3. She struggles with excessive reassurance seeking.
>
> Avery can hardly begin or perform a task without looking to an adult to ensure that he/she is pleased with what Avery is doing. She asks constant questions and needs to know if her work is good enough. She gets caught up in what others are doing, but focuses more on comparing her work to that of others and how others might perceive her work.
>
> *Ignore*
> You kindly answer a few of Avery's reassurance-seeking questions. Then you move on to another student and do not engage with Avery as she asks you more questions.
>
> *React*
> Avery's questions cause you to become agitated and distressed. They are off-topic and they disturb the other children. You tell Avery to focus on doing her work instead of asking for praise.
>
> *Respond*
> Understand that Avery's questions are based in her anxiety. Your focus should not be on preventing her repetitive questions but on the underlying insecurity and desire for perfection that are the root of this problem. Work with Avery to replace her questions with a more effective calming strategy.

During every social engagement and emotional interaction, we can help our students break down their thinking in order to understand its impact on their mood and behavior. We can help students become more aware of the way they interpret situations and the result those interpretations have on the actions they take. Positive thinking can be taught, nurtured, and developed with guidance and support. Neural-plasticity allows experience to develop new pathways in the brain and lets us learn new ways of thinking and feeling.

> **Teacher–Teacher Relationship**
>
> It can be challenging to be around someone who is always negative. Some people like to complain and see the problems in each situation. Be aware that a negative person might already know this about him/herself and might be working on it. When fellow teachers complain about a situation, consider how you can truly be most helpful to these colleagues and friends. Should you complain along with them and add other problems for them to consider? Should you tell them how right they are and that they should not put up with such a terrible situation? You might need to do this if the situation is a major problem and you see that they need to take drastic steps. However, if the problem is of moderate size, it might be more helpful if you encourage them to see the positives of the situation and to try a different way of thinking and feeling about the situation. You could list, say, three positive things about the situation instead of agreeing with all the negatives.

Ability-Building Activity

We can support children in changing the way they feel by changing the way they think. Rethinking is about actively trying to catch negative beliefs when they are exhibited and switch them into positive beliefs. It is about choosing not to listen to negative thinking, choosing to disagree with it and replace it with positive thoughts. It is an active effort to stop following the negative thinking, to catch it, and to fight the thoughts.

1. Use the Changing Thinking chart below and brainstorm examples with students.

CHANGING THINKING

Catch worried thinking and switch it to calm thinking	
Typical anxious thoughts: • *Something bad is going to happen.* • *I can't do this.* • *I'm not sure what I should do.* • *I must have done something wrong.* • *I wonder if they noticed that I made that mistake.*	Students can be encouraged to think in a positive way: • *I can do it.* • *It will be okay.*
Catch depressed thinking and switch it to happy thinking	
Typical depressed thoughts: • *No one likes me.* • *It will never work out for me.* • *I am not good at anything.* • *I am a failure.* • *It is hopeless.* • *I am not good enough.*	Students can be encouraged to think positively: • *I am a good person.* • *People know I am a good person.*
Catch angry thinking and switch it to forgiving thinking	
Typical angry thoughts: • *It is not fair.* • *Things never work out for me.* • *Other people get more than I do.* • *It is their fault.*	Students can be encouraged to think positively: • *This situation is not as bad as I think it is.* • *It's nobody's fault.*

2. Have students think of something they find hard to do or deal with. You can list various triggers on the board and refer back to the Trigger List on page 43.
3. Draw a stick figure on the board. Under it, write a situation or problem with the students. Brainstorm and write down negative thinking that the person in the situation could do. Link thinking with feeling: *How would you feel if you engaged in the negative thinking?*
4. Now have them change the thinking into something positive. Brainstorm how positive thinking would change the way they feel.
5. Refer to the two-part Problem Continuum (pages 104 and 105) to rate the size of the problem, having them fill in their thoughts, feelings, and actions: *If you think negatively, how big will the problem seem? If you think positively, how big will the problem seem?*

Problem Continuum: Part 1

Name: _____

Describe your situation or problem:
_____
_____

What size problem is this? Mark it on the scale.

Small   Medium   Large

Pembroke Publishers ©2014 *Stop the Stress in Schools* by Joey Mandel ISBN 978-1-55138-298-2

Problem Continuum: Part 2

I can think positively.

Name: _____

Describe your situation or problem:
_____
_____

What size problem is this? Mark it on the scale.

Small   Medium   Large
_____

If I think positively, my problem does not seem so big.

The Positive Response Process

Give Feedback

Have students examine their thinking during challenging situations and describe how their thinking is making a problem worse. They can use their Problem Continuum (page 104) to identify how severe the problem was when it started and how it got worse as they continued to think about it instead of using strategies.

Set Goals

Students learn to use positive thinking strategies to change the size of a problem.

Regulate

Begin to assist students in noticing the benefits of self-calming strategies: "Observe how you feel as you fight the negative thinking and decrease the size of a problem. Your body looks more relaxed and calmer. Do you feel softer, smoother, more in control? Is that a nice feeling?"

Engage

Be sure to be present with students and continue to listen to them. Students will not be able to shut off negative thinking immediately. If students persist in negative thinking, allow them to express their thoughts out loud. Do not be quick to dispute their statements. Listen and prompt with questions that might motivate them to seek a positive strategy: "That must feel frustrating. How does that thought make you feel? We could try to replace that negative thought with a positive thought and see if we feel better."

Support

Superheroes and animals are excellent images to invoke in strategies. It is helpful if students can draw upon the strength of others to gather strength in themselves; for example, detail for a student what Spiderman might tell himself to go out and face evil villains, or what salmon does to swim upriver.

Changing the Way Others Feel

Objectives: To learn how our behaviors influence others.

> Twenty minutes after every recess is taken up with handling interpersonal fighting between students. Every day, a different student is crying and a different leader seems to have emerged.
>
> *Ignore*
> You try to sort out each incident and get started on your lesson.
>
> *React*
> You tell students that there will be serious consequences to exclusion and bullying.
>
> *Respond*
> Before recess, sit with students and come up with a play plan that includes specific roles for specific students.

We all have the ability to raise up other people and make them feel good about themselves, or to put them down and make them feel bad about themselves. We must help students see that this is true not only in extreme cases of bullying and violent behavior, but also in the small, daily interactions within each of our relationships.

If a child sees that he/she has upset another child, the child can continue to do what is upsetting his/her peer, or can modify his/her behavior to change the way the other child feels. This seems like a given; however, it can be harder to change behavior than we think. If we build a strong community in our classrooms, if we consistently examine the behaviors of students and their impact on peers, we can begin to create a positive culture in the classroom.

> ### Teacher–Class Relationship
>
> Creating a strong classroom community begins by ensuring we are on top of the relationships between our students. We must follow up on the small interactions and dynamics, and make sure that we promote positive interactions. When we focus on tangible, positive, daily actions, we communicate to our students that what they do has effect on their classmates and the class as a whole. Catch and comment when students listen to each other, praise each other, and help each other; for example, "That was thoughtful and caring of you. You saw that Billy dropped his glue and you went over and picked it up for him. Thank you for helping build our positive community."

Ability-Building Activities

Charting Behavior

1. Create charts in the classroom to explicitly link positive behavior to positive impact on fellow students.

SAMPLE POSITIVE BEHAVIOR CHART

Positive Behavior	Positive Impact on My Classmates
Smile at three people today.	Three people will feel happy.
Compliment someone for what they have done: e.g., "Nice shot!"	Make someone feel happy.
Hold the door open for the person behind me.	The person feels noticed.
Someone drops a paper on the ground and I bend down and pick it up.	The person feels helped.

2. Make charts that link the impact of negative comments on how another person feels.

SAMPLE NEGATIVE BEHAVIOR CHART

Negative Behavior	Negative Impact on My Classmates
Make a negative comment: e.g., "Your shirt looks funny."	The person feels embarrassed.
Insult someone: e.g., "You are a terrible partner."	The person feels ashamed.
Exclude someone: e.g., "I don't want to be on your team."	The person feels sad.
Insult someone for something they have done: e.g. "You should have done your presentation differently."	The person feels annoyed.
I forget to hold the door open for the person behind me and let it slam in his/her face.	The person feels invisible.
I walk by someone and bang into him/her.	The person feels unimportant.

Mood Continuum

With the class, make a mood continuum; see page 109.

1. On the lines under left side of the continuum, add negative moods. On the lines in the centre of the continuum, add moderate feelings and moods. On the lines on the right side of the continuum, add positive moods.
2. Supply simple Happen/Think/Feel forms for students to record situations they want to talk about; see page 110. Enforce a no-name policy for this activity. Students write about their challenges without including the names of other students; students can comment anonymously.
3. Place the Mood Continuum and the blank Happen/Think/Feel forms in the hallway outside your classroom. Students can take from or add to the scale, especially when they come in from recess. They can place their filled-in forms on the chart in the appropriate place on the continuum, and can comment on the forms of their peers as well.

This activity allows students to express their challenges. It also allows them to see that other students are upset about the same issues. Finally, a student can read about what is upsetting other students and making them feel badly. If they recognize that their behavior is causing distress, they can be motivated to attempt to modify that behavior.

The Positive Response Process

Give Feedback

Encourage students' understanding that they have the power to affect the happiness of fellow students; they can make a friend feel good or they can make a

Mood Continuum

Happy
Excited
Thrilled

Good
Content
Okay

Angry
Irritated
Furious

Happen/Think/Feel

This is what happened:

This is what I thought:

This is what I felt:

Comments from Other Students:
☐ This has happened to me.
I think you should do this:

Self-Control

Name: _____ Date: _____

I stopped myself from saying something that would have hurt my partner's feelings: ☐ No
   ☐ Yes

I did this by _____

_____

I stayed seated and completed a task   ☐ No
   ☐ Yes

even though _____

Self-Control Rubric

Name: _____ Date: _____

Self-Control	
Level	To control my body and voice
1	• I did not stop moving; I did not look at members of my group. • I did not stop talking; I did not listen to members of my group.
2	• I tried to stop talking over members of my group. • I tried to stop moving so I could listen to members of my group.
3	• I looked and listened to members of my group. • I stayed engaged in the topic.
4	• I stayed there for the whole activity. • I stayed engaged in the topic. • I listened to everyone's ideas first, before I expressed mine. • I did not interrupt members of my group.

– –

Date: _____

Last class, I got a Level _____ because I _____

This class, I would like to get a Level _____. To do this, I will try to _____

_____

friend feel sad. In a gentle and nonjudgmental tone, link negative actions to the way other students feel.

Set Goals

Students can attempt each day to use self-control to prevent themselves from saying or doing something that will make a fellow classmate feel upset, irritated, or sad. Assist them in using the Self-Control sheet on page 110 and the Self-Control Rubric on page 111 for self-reflection. Students can complete the forms independently to give themselves feedback and set goals.

Regulate

Assist students in understanding that when we are in states of heightened stress we are more likely to snap at someone or say something unkind. As we begin to get upset, agitated, restless, tense, or strained in our bodies, our brains need to focus immediately on ourselves. We must try to relieve our inner stress, instead of looking outward at what someone else is doing or saying and taking out our negative feelings on them.

Progressive muscle relaxation is a healthy alternative way to release negative tension and helps students gain control over their bodies. Guide students through progressive muscle relaxation: *Tense and relax your muscles by doing the following:*

- *Open your mouth/shut your mouth.*
- *Scrunch your cheeks/relax your cheeks.*
- *Open your eyes wide/close your eyes tightly.*
- *Squeeze your face/relax your face.*
- *Point your toes/flex your toes.*
- *Tighten your body/relax your body.*

Engage

Be present and encourage students to distract their brains from what or who is upsetting them. Guide them away from that classmate. Look students in the eyes and prompt them to distract their brains. Tell them that they are stuck right now in being mad at a classmate. Remind them that, before saying things they might regret, they can focus their brain energy on themselves.

Support

Allow students to express themselves to you. Let a student express what he/she wants to say to other students to you instead, even yelling it out. Then ask the student to go through progressive muscle relaxation with you. After the activity, encourage the student to express the same information to you again. Discuss with the student the different tone in his/her voice and way that he/she looked while talking. Was he/she more relaxed because he/she took a few minutes to self-calm?

Going Back and Trying Again

Objective: To build perseverance and resilience through exposure to challenges and adversity.

When using the Self-Control Rubric on page 111, students complete the top section immediately after an activity. The bottom half of the sheet is to be completed before a new activity, usually on another day. Encourage students to read over their previous self-evaluation and to set themselves new goals.

Yelling, snapping, and screaming are unhealthy ways of self-calming and relieving negative emotions like anger or anxiety. These actions often release the body's tension, but there are negative consequences to this way of self-calming.

> Muhammad is in Grade 2. He struggles with fear of dogs.
>
> Muhammad loves to play inside the classroom and likes gym class. However, it is becoming increasingly difficult to get Muhammad to go outside at recess and impossible to get him to go for outdoor physical education. This pattern of behavior started the day the gym teacher took the class outdoors for soccer and there were large dogs on the field. The dogs' owners where very slow to move their dogs off the field, and the gym teacher needed to ask them to leash their dogs several times.
>
> *Ignore*
> You ask the gym teacher not to take the class outside until you can speak with your principal and ensure that the school is a dog-free zone.
>
> *React*
> You tell Muhammad that he needs to go outside for recess and for gym class. You explain to him that, over time, he will get over this worry.
>
> *Respond*
> Understand that Muhammad has a phobia that, with hard work, can be conquered. For you to help him, he needs to understand that you realize how he feels and that you know the fear is real for him. Do not try to logically dismiss his fear or tell him what he should feel. Make a simple plan with Muhammad to figure out what he thinks he might need to be able to try going outside.

Students build skills by facing hard tasks, challenging problems, and difficult situations, and by seeing the work through to some degree of completion. As long as their experience with adversity is met with some form of success, then they might be able to go back and attempt the task once more. Success should not be viewed as only the perfect, flawless completion of a task. It does not mean that a student needs to get an A on a book report; it might mean that the student picked up a pencil and wrote a few sentences of the report. We need to consistently set up situations in which a student must face a task, start it, move through it, and reach some degree of completion in order to be able to celebrate his/her version of success.

Without achieving some degree of positive success from a task or experience, students can be apprehensive about attempting again; this can start a vicious cycle of avoidance and fear. The very avoidance of a task or experience increases the experience of the fear; the temporary relief from avoiding a task makes a student feel safe and relaxed. The student learns that avoidance feels like safety, and fears the act of attempting itself.

Managing difficult thoughts and emotions builds resilience.

Exposure to challenges with a positive view to success is an effective way of decreasing fears. Successful exposure includes any attempt to face the fear, begin a task, move through it, and have some degree of closure. Children face events that elicit negative thoughts ("I can't do it") and feelings (fear, worry); however, if they experience success in attempting the task, they begin to realize that they have the capacity to face their challenges. With some degree of closure, a child is likely to be willing to come back another day and try again, which is how children build the traits of perseverance and resilience.

If we overprotect children from challenges it sends a message that they are not capable of handling them. It reduces their ability to practice facing hard tasks and using their skills and talents to overcome a problem, which is how they overcome negative thoughts and feelings. Without experience in managing difficult thoughts and emotions, they do not have the ability to persevere through hard tasks or to face adversity and bounce back to try again.

> ### Teacher–Parent Relationship
>
> Some parents overprotect and rush in to save their children from making mistakes or experiencing any failure. By protecting their children from little problems, they are not allowing them to experience the challenges in school that, once overcome, build confidence and trust in oneself to be able to handle future challenges. Make active attempts to get parents on board with you in building resilience in their children. If parents trust their child's teacher and believe that the teacher will assist the child through challenges, then they might be less inclined to overprotect their child. Send a message home that, as parents, they can let their children fail, that you will be there to support the children if they need you.

Ability-Building Activities

We want to assist students in facing a challenging task, persevering through it, and coming back to try again after unsuccessful exposures. So it is important to explore with students the thinking that is preventing them from approaching the task or activity, and to help them reflect on their worries so that they can consider the severity of the situation. Exploring "what-if" situations and thinking and talking about what could happen if things go badly are essential discussions to have with students to encourage them to explore how they can decrease the impact of a trigger:

- *What can you do to minimize the impact of a bad situation? Or the bad action on the part of another person? Or a scary task you have to do?*
- *What if you go to read in front of the class and you end up getting stuck on a few words that are hard? Would that be so bad? Has something like that happened to other students in the class? Was it the end of the world? Are you still friends with them?*
- *What if you go out for recess and your friends are mad at you and talking about you behind your back? This upsetting situation could act as a trigger. It could get you upset and begin a negative cycle of thinking against yourself or against your friends. It might make you think that they are mean. It might make you feel upset, sad, or angry. But what if this does happen? Is this the kind of thing that happens to other people—children and adults? How do other people handle this? What thinking can we use to minimize how we feel about this?*

1. Have students brainstorm different examples of problems that could occur at school: for example, doing poorly on a test, hurting a friend, losing an important piece of paper, not making a school team. Choose one example as a class.
2. Draw a Problem Continuum (see page 44) on the interactive whiteboard. Rate the problem as a class. Accept that students will likely not agree, so consider with the class how you will choose together, even if some students disagree with the level chosen.
3. Discuss actions that they could take to make the problem bigger or smaller.

4. Draw a chart with students. Label the left side *I Can Make the Problem Bigger* and label the right side *I Can Make the Problem Smaller*. Have students brainstorm different ways to increase and decrease the size of a problem.

SAMPLE OF MAKING A PROBLEM BIGGER/SMALLER

I can make a problem bigger by…	I can make a problem smaller by…
• running away • hitting someone • hiding • lying • making up a story • yelling • blaming someone else	• changing how I think • controlling my actions • accepting responsibility • saying I'm sorry • proposing a solution • fixing my mistake • explaining how I will change my behavior

5. Using the I Have a Problem template on page 116, have students consider a problem they have encountered at school. Ask them to rate the problem and to chart how they would make the problem bigger or smaller.

The Positive Response Process

Give Feedback

Explicitly explain to students that you will encourage them to start tasks and face hurdles that they might want to run away from. Tell them that if they learn to push through things they think are hard, these things might become easier. Invite students to identify their triggers and to create a Fear Ladder, or a list of related events ranked in terms of fear from lowest to highest.

SAMPLE FEAR LADDER

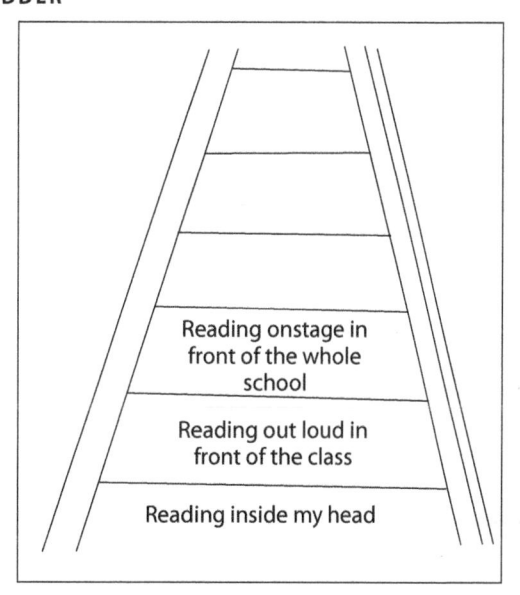

Reading onstage in front of the whole school

Reading out loud in front of the class

Reading inside my head

I Have a Problem

Name: _____

Describe your problem:
_____
_____

Rate the size of your problem:

1   5   10

Draw a picture of how you made your problem bigger. Draw a picture of how you made your problem smaller.

I can make a problem bigger	I can make a problem smaller

Rate your problem after you made your problem bigger.

1   5   10

Rate your problem after you made your problem smaller.

1   5   10

Pembroke Publishers ©2014 *Stop the Stress in Schools* by Joey Mandel ISBN 978-1-55138-298-2

Set Goals

Work with students to set a time frame and an exposure plan to try things they are afraid of.

Regulate

Understand that before students face a difficult challenge they will be distracted and might not be able to focus on other lessons of the day. Instead of pushing students to focus on your lesson, encourage them to use a self-calming technique.

Engage

Allow students outlets to express their thoughts and worries about a difficult challenge they fear; for example, have them write in their Thinking and Feeling journals. Give students time to talk or write about what they are thinking and feeling. Note that allotting a precise amount of time for this will help them contain and control their thinking.

Support

Understand that the anxiety students feel in anticipation of an event is often worse than the anxiety they experience when actually facing the event. If you notice that a student is experiencing increased distress thinking about an upcoming event, consider ways to make the event happen sooner so that the student has less time to worry about the event, or ways to distract the student with an enjoyable activity before the event.

Applying Strategies

Objective: To build motivation to apply strategies independently and in different settings.

> Gabe is in Grade 6.
>
> You have had many meetings with Gabe's parents. This time you had to call them because it has been another hard week, with Gabe insulting and even pushing other students in the class. He often snaps at his classmates and is quick to tell them what he does not like about them. Gabe's parents are distraught. They see none of these behaviors at home, where he gets along rather well with his sister and is generally an easy child to raise.
>
> *Ignore*
> You have a chat with Gabe's parents and ask them to talk with Gabe at home. You advise them to tell him that he needs to behave at school as well as he does at home.
>
> *React*
> You tell Gabe that he will need to improve his behavior at school or he will not be able to go on the class trip.
>
> *Respond*
> Discuss with Gabe's parents what Gabe typically does at home and how he responds to them or his sister when he is upset. Bring Gabe into the discussion and gather his input as to what steps he could take to use the same strategies at school that he does at home.

Students who are innately able to apply self-calming strategies are able to mitigate the impact of stress in the moment, and so are less likely to engage in actions or behaviors that get them into challenging situations with themselves and others. Over time, we want students not only to be willing to try the strategies, but also ultimately to apply these strategies consistently and independently in various settings.

For students to be independently motivated to apply strategies on their own, they need to connect with and internalize new ways of managing their thinking and feeling. Children who notice a positive physiological transformation when they stop and ground themselves, when they breathe deeply, when they visualize something meaningful, and when they actively attempt to rethink a negative situation are more likely to engage in the process again. Without an awareness of the process, they will be less likely to turn to it in times of need. Each successive time they feel a reduction of the physiological symptoms they experience from stress, they experience aggregate success and feel increased inclination and ability to engage in the strategy again.

Use positive vocabulary to assist students in connecting their efforts in self-calming with their physical decrease in stress: "Your body looks light/free/relaxed/calm/gentle/soothed."

Students actually gain in ability to engage in the process, because the self-calming strategies we teach them alter the pathways in their brains. Just like physical exercise, these techniques, if used repeatedly over time, strengthen the pathways that release biochemicals in our brains that send messages to the body to soothe and quiet our senses.

This is not quick process. It not only takes a long time to learn, practice, and apply, but also works only if students are able and willing to practice regularly. While we hope that students will eventually choose to use the strategies on their own for their intrinsic benefits, we can attempt to motivate students to be willing to be part of the process by breaking down their involvement into discrete tasks and by celebrating their successes. You might even consider rewarding students who really struggle with big reactions and big feelings for trying to practice the strategies, even outside of the moment. It is likely that the students who resist learning the techniques are the ones who need to learn them the most. It is worth developing a reward system for these students in order to expose them to the process.

Teacher–Class Relationship

Many educators criticize the implementation of reward charts, but some students need external motivators to get on board and participate in a process. For these students, small, tangible demands linked closely with small, tangible rewards can have huge benefits.

Unfair reward systems impose a huge, broad demand for a future reward; for example, "If you behave well for the month, you can have an afternoon party on the last Friday of every month." It will be impossible for students to experience success in these conditions. What makes good behavior is not defined in this system and, at some point in the month, it is likely that many students will not behave well.

Conditions that are very specific and immediate will result in more success; for example, "You can practice the STOP activity any time during guided reading today. If you check off that you have completed it, then we can play our game before we go out for recess."

---

118   *Ability to Manage Stress*

Ability-Building Activity

Lead students in a meditation.
- *Stop.*
- *Plant your feet into the ground.*
- *Take a slow deep breath.*
- *Push your feet harder into the ground and breathe in again.*
- *Continue to breathe as you push your feet against the ground.*
- *Now imagine something from your Happy Box. Imagine one thing that you have, a picture of someone special or something that you do that makes you feel happy on the inside, that makes you smile.*
- *Continue to breathe.*
- *Scrunch up your body as tight as you can. Feel tightness in your face, shoulders, and body.*
- *Now picture your special something and release your body, relaxing your face, shoulders, and body.*
- *Continue breathing slowly, letting the air come in slowly and releasing it slowly.*
- *Feel the connection between releasing your tension and your special happy something.*
- *If you take control of your body, your breathing, and your thinking, you can begin to change the way you think and feel. You have the power to do that. You have the power to control how you feel.*

For more on Happy Boxes, see page 97.

The Positive Response Process

Give Feedback

Have students examine their behavior and perseverance when they are playing their favorite game or participating in an activity they love. Encourage them to detail the amount of energy they have and the different ways they will problem-solve and use strategies if something that they enjoy doing is not working.

Set Goals

Students will come to understand that they have strong resourcefulness, motivation, and resilience abilities for activities that they enjoy. They must begin to apply those same traits to areas and activities that they find challenging.

Regulate

Regulation is not always about calming down and decreasing energy levels. When children are engaged in tasks they dislike, they become disengaged or apathetic. Their energy levels tend to be low and they lack the motivation to lean in, begin, push through, and complete a task. Inspire students to build up their energy levels by initiating activities that get the body moving, like jumpingjacks or running.

Engage

Try to avoid telling students what to do; instead, prompt them through gentle questioning, reminding them of their inner tools. For example, say, "What do you think you could do?" or "Remember what you did during recess to chase negative thoughts away?"

Support

Teach students to independently transfer their positive thinking—"I can do it" and "I can handle this"—from one activity to another, and from one environment to another.

Conclusion

When we focus on building essential social-emotional character traits, strong and healthy relationships with self and others will emerge. We can begin by promoting and teaching traits like kindness and respect, but if we take the extra step of addressing the traits of stress awareness, acceptance, and ability to manage stress, both students and teachers will gain the skills to be kind and respectful, even during challenging moments.

As teachers, we can begin to focus on character traits first for ourselves to assist us as we navigate the stressful challenges of our personal lives, work demands, and student needs. As we become aware of our reactions and the patterns in which we think, feel, and behave, we can model for our students appropriate ways of skilfully managing and reducing stress. The lasting result will be more controlled responses to our students from us as teachers, and in turn from our students, and the creation of stronger and healthier relationships and classroom communities.

Acknowledgments

At Pembroke, I would like to thank my ever-encouraging publisher Mary Macchiusi, whose e-mails always put a smile on my face, and Kat Mototsune, who brilliantly brought the whole book together. I would also like to express my appreciation to Hannah Sung, not only for taking my picture for the book, but for pushing me as a writer by questioning my intent and capturing my message; to my good friend Ilaria Sheikh at the B.E.N. School, who has dedicated her life to creating a kind and gentle school community; to my mom, who is always there for me; and to my dad, the first person I call when I want to discuss a topic in depth or if I want someone to challenge my assumptions. Thanks to Mike, Joshua, and Tyler for bringing joy to my life.

Professional Resources

Bessell, Harold (1972) *Human Development Program: Activity Guide Level III*. Spring Valley, CA: Palomares and Associates.
Briers, Stephen (2009) *Brilliant Cognitive Behavioural Therapy*. Toronto, ON: Pearson Prentice Hall.
Brookhart, Susan M. (2008) *How To Give Effective Feedback To Your Students*. Alexandria, VA: Association for Supervision and Curriculum Development.
Crooke, Pamela and Winner, Michelle Garcia (2011) *Social Fortune or Social Fate*. San Jose, CA: Social Thinking Publishing.
Greenberger, Dennis and Padesky, Christine (1995) *Mind Over Mood*. New York, NY: Guilford Press.
Greene, Ross (2005) *The Explosive Child*. New York, NY: HarperCollins.
Heegaard, Marge Eaton (2001) *Drawing Together to Learn about Feelings*. Minneapolis, MN: Fairview Press.
Heegaard, Marge Eaton (2001) *Drawing Together to Learn about Self-Control*. Minneapolis, MN: Fairview Press.
Huebner, Dawn (2007) *What to Do When You Grumble Too Much*. Washington, DC: Magination Press.
Kendall, Philip C. and Hedtke, Kristina A. (2006) *The Coping Cat Workbook*. Chattanooga, TN: Workbook Publishing.
Madrigal, Stephanie and Winner, Michelle Garcia (2008) *Superflex®: A Superhero Social Thinking Curriculum Package*. San Jose, CA: Social Thinking Publishing.
Mandel, Joey (2013) *Moment to Moment: A Positive Approach to Managing Classroom Behavior*. Markham, ON: Pembroke.
Matthews, Bonnie (2006) *What to Do When You Worry Too Much: A Kid's Guide to Overcoming Anxiety (What to Do Guides for Kids)*. Washington, DC: Magination Press.
Melrose, Regalena (2013) *The Sixty Seconds Fix*. Long Beach, CA: 60 Seconds Press.
Ministry of Education (2013) *Supporting Minds: An Educator's Guide to Promoting Students' Mental Health and Well-being*, Draft Version. Toronto, ON: The Ontario Public Service.
Molyneux, Lynn (1996) *Measuring Success*. Middle Grove, NY: Trellis Books.
Palomares, Uvaldo and Dunne, Gerry (1988) *Magic Circle. A Program for Developing Self-Concept, Self-Esteem and Social Responsibility*. Spring Valley, CA: Palomares and Associates.
Pepler, Debra (2006) "Bullying Interventions: A Binocular Perspective" *Canadian Academy of Child & Adolescent Psychiatry*, 15(1): 16–20 at http://www.ncbi.nlm.nih.gov/pmc/articles/PMC2277273/

Ratey, John J. and Johnson, Catherine (1997) *Shadow Syndromes.* New York, NY: Pantheon.

Schmitz, Connie and Hipp, Earl (1987) *A Teacher's Guide to Fighting Invisible Tigers: A 12-Part Course In Lifeskills Development.* Minneapolis, MN: Free Spirit Publishing Co.

Shanker, Stuart (2013) *Calm, Alert, and Learning: Classroom Strategies for Self-Regulation.* Toronto, ON: Pearson.

Szpirglas, Jeff (2006) *Fear This Book. Your Guide to Fright, Horror, & Things That Go Bump in the Night.* Toronto, ON: Maple Tree Press.

Vgotsky, Lev S. (1986) *Thought and Language,* Revised Edition. Cambridge, MA: MIT Press.

Waddell, C., Offord, D.R., Shepherd, C.A., Hua, J.M., and McEwan, K. (2002) "Child psychiatric epidemiology and Canadian public policy-making: The state of the science and the art of the possible" *Canadian Journal of Psychiatry*, 47: 825–32.

Wagner, Aureen (2008) *CBT for OCD and Anxiety in Children & Adolescents* (workshop).

Winner, Michelle (2010) *Social Behavior Mapping: Connecting Behavior, Emotions and Consequences Across the Day.* San Jose, CA: Social Thinking Publishing.

Winner, Michelle (2007) *Thinking about YOU Thinking about ME*, 2nd edition. San Jose, CA: Social Thinking Publishing.

Winner, Michelle (2005) *Think Social! A Social Thinking Curriculum for School-Age Students.* San Jose, CA: Social Thinking Publishing.

Young-Eisendrath, Polly (2008) *the self-esteem trap.* New York, NY: Little, Brown and Company.

Index

ability-building activities
    applying strategies, 119
    changing the way others feel, 107–108
    changing the way we think, 103
    going back and trying again, 114–115
    self-calming, 97–98
ability to manage stress
    applying strategies, 117–120
    changing the way others feel, 106–112
    changing the way we think, 102–106
    described, 26, 95
    going back and trying again, 112–117
    self-calming, 95–101
acceptance
    of the behavior of others, 90–94
    described, 26, 67
    of the need to adapt, 85–89
    of others, 69–72
    of self, 67–69
    of the situation, 72–77
    of the thinking of others, 77–84
acceptance-building activities
    behavior of others, 91
    need to adapt, 86–87
    others, 70–71
    self, 68
    situation, 73–75
    thinking of others, 78–81
accepting others' behavior, 90–92
amygdala, 7
anger, 70
anxiety, 117
applying strategies, 117–120
awareness
    of challenges, 33–36
    described, 26, 27
    of impact of stress on behavior, 51–56
    of impact of stress on body, 45–51
    of impact of stress on feelings, 60–66
    of impact of stress on thinking, 56–60
    of others' strengths and challenges, 36–38
    of strengths, 27–32
    of triggers, 39–44
awareness-building activities
    challenges, 34–35
    impact of stress on behavior, 53–54
    impact of stress on body, 45–47
    impact of stress on feelings, 61–62
    impact of stress on thinking, 57–58
    others' strengths and challenges, 37
    strengths, 29–30
    triggers, 40–41

Behavior Mapping, 86
Behavior Mood chart, 75
Behavior Tracking, 86–87, 89
    sample, 88
Body Stress Curve, 50, 51
breathing activity, 41, 62, 97

Calm Down bench, 71
Challenge chart, 34–35
challenges,
    others, 36–38
    self, 33–36
Change: Drawing chart, 91, 93
Change: Writing chart, 91, 94
changing the way others feel, 106–112
changing the way we think, 102–106
Changing Thinking chart, 103
character traits
    basic, 25
    social-emotional, 25–26
charting
    behavior, 107–108
    positive experiences, 22
classroom community, 107
community circles, 37

Compromise chart, 87
Conflict Resolution, 80, 84
Conflict Resolution Checklist, 79, 82
conflict-resolution mediation, 78–80
consequences, 9–10
Control chart, 91
core beliefs, 34, 57, 90

deep breathing, 41, 62, 97
distracting one's brain, 112
dopamine, 52

engaging, 23
    accepting others, 72
    accepting others' behavior, 92
    applying strategies, 119
    challenges, 35
    changing the way others feel, 112
    changing the way we think, 106
    going back and trying again, 117
    impact of stress on behavior, 56
    impact of stress on body, 51
    impact of stress on feelings, 62
    impact of stress on thinking, 59–60
    need to adapt, 88
    others' strengths and challenges, 38
    self-acceptance, 69
    self-calming, 99
    situational acceptance, 77
    strengths, 31
    thinking of others, 81
    triggers, 42
explosive behavior, 52
exposure to challenges, 113
expressing oneself, 38, 79–80, 106, 108, 112, 117

fairness, 70, 90
Fear Ladder, 115
fear response, 6
feedback, 21
    accepting others, 71
    accepting others' behavior, 91
    applying strategies, 119
    challenges, 35
    changing the way others feel, 108, 112
    changing the way we think, 106
    chart, 30
    going back and trying again, 115
    impact of stress on behavior, 55
    impact of stress on body, 47
    impact of stress on feelings, 62
    impact of stress on thinking, 59
    need to adapt, 87
    others' strengths and challenges, 37–38
    self-acceptance, 69
    self-calming, 99
    situational acceptance, 75
    strengths, 30
    thinking of others, 81
    triggers, 41
Fight, Flight, or Freeze reaction, 7, 22, 45, 52, 96, 99
flexible thinking, 85

goal setting, 21–22
    accepting others, 71
    accepting others' behavior, 92
    applying strategies, 119
    challenges, 35
    changing the way others feel, 112
    changing the way we think, 106
    going back and trying again, 117
    impact of stress on behavior, 56
    impact of stress on body, 51
    impact of stress on feelings, 62
    impact of stress on thinking, 59
    need to adapt, 87
    others' strengths and challenges, 38
    self-acceptance, 69
    self-calming, 99
    situational acceptance, 77
    strengths, 30
    thinking of others, 81
    triggers, 41
going back and trying again, 112–117
grounding activity, 97
guiding principles, 19

Happen/Think/Feel, 108, 110
Happy Boxes, 97–98, 119
high stress, 7, 45, 96
Hot Thoughts, 57

I Have a Problem, 115, 116
ignorance approach, 19
interpersonal dynamics, 12

low stress, 7

Making a Problem Bigger/Smaller chart, 115
mediators, 78–80
meditation, 119
medium stress, 7, 8

mental health strategies, 8–9
mistake, 71
Mood Chart, 63
Mood Continuum, 108, 109
moods, 60
My Energy Level, 47, 49
My Stress Curve, 48

need to adapt, 85–89
Negative Behavior chart, 108
negative self-awareness, 33
negative thinking, 15, 57–62, 73, 75, 91, 103, 106, 113–114
negative thought record, 58
Negative Thoughts chart, 61, 68
neocortex, 7, 52
neural-plasticity, 102
noticing activity, 98
Noticing During an Activity, 98, 100
Noticing Through the Day, 98, 101

Observations and Conclusions, 73–74, 76
overprotection, 113–114

peer-to-peer mediation, 81
perseverance, 112–117
personal strengths, 27–32
personal stress, 9
Positive Action chart, 29–30
Positive Behavior chart, 107
positive classroom, 9, 11–12, 58, 78
Positive Feedback chart, 30
positive response, 18
positive response process
  accepting others, 71–72
  accepting others' behavior, 91–92
  applying strategies, 119–120
  challenges, 35–36
  changing the way others feel, 108, 112
  changing the way we think, 106
  described, 20–21
  engaging, 23
  feedback, 21
  goal setting, 21–22
  going back and trying again, 115, 117
  impact of stress on behavior, 54–56
  impact of stress on body, 47, 51
  impact of stress on feelings, 62
  impact of stress on thinking, 59–60
  need to adapt, 87–88
  others' strengths and challenges, 37–38
  regulating, 22–23
  sample, 24
  self-acceptance, 69
  self-calming, 99
  situational acceptance, 75, 77
  steps, 21
  strengths, 30–31
  supporting, 23
  thinking of others, 81
  triggers, 41–42
Positive Scale, 21–22
positive self-talk, 15, 23, 34, 68, 71, 74, 78, 87, 90, 98
positive thinking, 57, 59–61, 102–103, 106
Positive Thoughts chart, 61
positive vocabulary, 118
Problem Continuum, 44, 103, 104–105, 106, 114
Problem Scales, 41
problem-solving, 19, 23
professional development, 6
progressive muscle relaxation, 112
proximal support, 42

Question chart, 53
questioning, 53

reactionary approach, 19
reactive strategies, 6
Ready for Mediation, 80, 83
regulating, 22–23
  accepting others, 71
  accepting others' behavior, 92
  applying strategies, 119
  challenges, 35
  changing the way others feel, 112
  changing the way we think, 106
  going back and trying again, 117
  impact of stress on behavior, 56
  impact of stress on body, 51
  impact of stress on feelings, 62
  impact of stress on thinking, 59
  need to adapt, 88
  others' strengths and challenges, 38
  self-acceptance, 69
  self-calming, 99
  situational acceptance, 77
  strengths, 30–31
  thinking of others, 81
  triggers, 41
relationship dynamics, 12
relationships
  schoolwide, 78

strong, 11
student, 14–17, 29, 34, 40, 75, 78, 81, 87, 90, 96
teacher, 12–14, 30, 37, 42, 52, 58, 61, 71, 72, 75, 86, 102, 107, 114, 118
resilience, 112–117
responding approach, 20
response, 21
response cycle, 18
reward charts, 118
rigid thinking, 85
rules, 11

safe space, 99
Say It/Don't Say It, 44
self-acceptance, 67–69
self-calming, 8, 22–23, 31, 35, 38, 51, 62, 88, 92, 95–99, 106, 117–118
  ability to manage stress, 95–99
  stop list of strategies, 80
self-control, 112
Self-Control chart, 111, 112
Self-Control Rubric, 111, 112
self-criticism, 69, 73
self-examination, 33, 36, 68
self-forgiveness, 67
self-reflection, 28, 30–34, 36, 38, 45–46, 71, 112
Self-Reflection Checklist, 32
situational acceptance, 72–77
social-emotional character traits
  ability to manage stress, 26, 95–120
  acceptance, 26, 67–94
  awareness, 26, 27–66
  chart, 29
  described, 25–26
starter questions, 37
Stop and Calm Down chart, 96
Stop list, 79, 82
  self-calming strategies, 51, 80
strengths,
  others, 36–38
  self, 27–32
stress
  ability to manage, 26, 95–120
  cycles, 52
  described, 6–7
  drawing body under, 46
  effect of, 6–8
  impact on behavior, 51–56
  impact on body, 45–51
  impact on feelings, 60–62
  impact on thinking, 56–60
  levels of, 7–8
  personal, 9
  physical symptoms, 47
  stopping, 9–10
  teaching, 6
  triggers, 6–7, 20, 40, 45, 96
Stress Curve, 7–8, 45
  Body Stress Curve, 50, 51
  sample, 46, 48, 99
Stress Makes Me…, 54, 55
student behavior
  acting on, 18–20
  ignoring, 19
  reacting to, 19
  responding to, 19, 20
student relationships, 11, 14–17
  class-student, 16–17
  student–class, 16, 29, 40, 78, 90
  student–self, 15, 34, 87
  student–student, 15–16, 75, 81, 96
Student Survey, 61, 64–65
supporting, 19, 23
  accepting others, 72
  accepting others' behavior, 92
  applying strategies, 120
  challenges, 36
  changing the way others feel, 112
  changing the way we think, 106
  going back and trying again, 117
  impact of stress on behavior, 56
  impact of stress on body, 51
  impact of stress on feelings, 62
  impact of stress on thinking, 60
  need to adapt, 88
  others' strengths and challenges, 38
  self-acceptance, 69
  self-calming, 99
  situational acceptance, 77
  strengths, 31
  thinking of others, 81
  triggers, 42

teacher relationships, 11, 12–14
  teacher–class, 13–14, 52, 71, 107, 118
  teacher–parent, 72, 114
  teacher–self, 12–13, 42, 58, 61, 86
  teacher–student, 14, 30
  teacher–teacher, 13, 37, 75, 102
Thinking and Feeling notebooks, 8, 56, 70, 117
thinking coach, 5
thinking of others, 77–81

thought records, 57–58, 68
   sample, 59
   student, 68
   teacher, 68
Thought-to-Mood for Teachers, 62, 66
Trigger List, 40, 43
triggers, 6–7, 20, 39–42, 45, 53–54, 96
   list, 42, 43, 53–54

visualizing activity, 97–98

What I Might Be Thinking, 59
"what-if" situations, 114

zone of proximal development, 20